NO ORDINARY PEOPLE

The
UNKNOWN MEN & WOMEN
of the Bible
DEVOTIONAL

DAVID McLAUGHLAN

BARBOUR BOOKS
An Imprint of Barbour Publishing, Inc.

© 2016 by David McLaughlan.

Print ISBN 978-1-63409-119-0

eBook Editions:
Adobe Digital Edition (.epub) 978-1-60742-576-2
Kindle and MobiPocket Edition (.prc) 978-1-60742-577-9

Scripture quotations marked KJV are taken from the King James Version of the Bible.

Scripture quotations marked NIV are taken from the HOLY BIBLE, NEW INTERNATIONAL VERSION®. NIV®. Copyright © 1973, 1978, 1984, 2011 by Biblica, Inc.™ Used by permission. All rights reserved worldwide.

Published by Barbour Books, an imprint of Barbour Publishing, Inc., P.O. Box 719, Uhrichsville, Ohio 44683, www.barbourbooks.com

Our mission is to publish and distribute inspirational products offering exceptional value and biblical encouragement to the masses.

ecpa Member of the
Evangelical Christian
Publishers Association

Printed in the United States of America.

INTRODUCTION

The followers of Christ are, of course, no ordinary people, but sometimes it seems like we have to live up to the examples set by the extra-ordinary role models in the Bible—kings and queens, miracle workers, the Son of God!

Of course, we *should* aspire to the highest of standards. It's just not always the easiest thing for flawed humans to do. So, if we are daunted by the prospect of following the examples set by David, Paul, Esther, and other major characters in the Bible, should we look elsewhere for role models?

No. There are plenty of "ordinary" people in the Bible, as well, and their very inclusion in the Good Book means they have a purpose to serve. Whether good, bad, or accidentally passing by, they are in the Bible because they have a message to share. They are no ordinary people.

Too often they get passed over in favor of more famous names. So here, for perhaps the first time, those anonymous men and women come to the forefront. Let's walk with them and talk with them and learn how we, as supposedly ordinary people ourselves, might also play important roles in God's plan.

POTIPHAR'S WIFE—
The Attraction of Purity

"No one is greater in this house than I am. My master has withheld nothing from me except you, because you are his wife. How then could I do such a wicked thing and sin against God?" And though she spoke to Joseph day after day, he refused to go to bed with her or even be with her.

GENESIS 39:9–10 NIV

As the wife of the captain of Pharaoh's guard, Potiphar's wife was in a privileged position—or was she?

Surely, when it came to food, fine clothes, and material goods, she would have been the envy of much of Egypt, but she seems to have been lacking in one very important thing. Her husband's love. No doubt he was a busy man. Serving Pharaoh (who was as close to being a pagan god as was possible for a human to be in those days) must have been his first priority and would have taken almost all his time.

So, in her loneliness or self-indulgence, she offered herself to Joseph, the head of her household slaves. No doubt Joseph was a handsome young man, but what probably attracted her to him the most—and what eventually infuriated her—was his purity. He could have settled for the easy life and kept his mistress happy, but as a faithful man of God, that was never going to happen. So, she accused him of rape and had him imprisoned. Which, of course, put him where God

> Lord, help us aspire to purity. Let us not be distracted along the way by the wiles of the world. And when we are attacked for our desire to be more like You— as we undoubtedly will be— help us understand that those who attack us are not role models to be followed but suffering souls who need Your love. May we be able to help them without following them. In Your mercy, amen.

wanted him—where he would come to the attention of Pharaoh.

But what of Potiphar's wife? Did she do what she did because she was simply wicked? Well, wickedness does have a penchant for purity. It will try, first, to corrupt it and then to destroy it. But there is a deeper level to that terrible attraction. Beneath the decadent, idolatrous lifestyle was a soul that longed to know God. Joseph would have been the closest thing to the true God in her world. But his purity shone a light on the lack of God and the lack of love in her life. It would have been in pain, wearing the mask of hate, that she lashed out.

What did Potiphar's wife really want? Not Joseph (although she was used by God to further his wonderful story). What she wanted was to know God's love as expressed on this earth by her husband's love for her. But he was busy serving an earthly god, and that's never the way to achieve lasting happiness, marital or otherwise.

MOSES' ETHIOPIAN WIFE—
An Excuse for Jealousy?

And Miriam and Aaron spake against Moses because of the Ethiopian woman whom he had married: for he had married an Ethiopian woman. And they said, Hath the LORD indeed spoken only by Moses? hath he not spoken also by us? And the LORD heard it.

NUMBERS 12:1–2 KJV

The identity of Moses' Ethiopian (or Cushite) wife is an open subject for scholarly debate—but not really the point of her inclusion in the Bible.

The Cushites were regarded as descendants of Noah but not children of Abraham, so such a marriage may have been cause for antagonism. The Bible does not mention *when* Moses married her. The Romano-Jewish historian Josephus refers to the Cushite woman as someone Moses married while in Egypt. Perhaps she was left in Egypt, perhaps she died there, or perhaps Moses took her as his wife at the time when he appeared to have sent Zipporah (his recognized wife and mother of his children) away. None of these are really the reason for mentioning her.

Miriam and Aaron, Moses' sister and brother, weren't happy with him, so they raised the issue of the Cushite marriage. Isn't it interesting how we use past or minor antagonisms to disguise our present, larger pains?

> Lord, we are prideful creatures. Even when desiring to do Your bidding, we like to think that we can do it better than anyone else. Lord, we might hope You put it down to an excess of zeal and turn a blind eye, but You do us a greater service when You sweep such conceits away. Keep us ever aware that You can raise servants from the rocks on the ground. In our humility may we better serve You.

Miriam went directly from criticizing the Cushite marriage to revealing the real reason for her unhappiness. God was working directly with Moses and not her. These days we might sympathize with that stance, but God Himself said He operates in different ways at different times. Sometimes He appeared to prophets in dreams, but at that moment, He was working through Moses. Who was Miriam to argue against that?

A leprous face (which we assume was cured after a period of cleansing) was her reminder that God will do what God will do.

What role the Cushite woman played in Moses' day-to-day life goes unrecorded, but her inclusion in this incident should remind us of two things. Firstly, sins (if this marriage was in any way sinful) once forgiven are forgotten by God. We ought to strive to do likewise and not resurrect old sins for our own selfish purposes. And, secondly, if someone is doing the work of God, then we ought to look for ways to build them up rather than find excuses to tear them down. If they are truly walking with God—as Moses undoubtedly was—then it's up to us to get alongside them and help rather than complain because God hasn't asked us to do what they are already doing.

THE WITCH OF ENDOR—
Saul Seeks God via the Devil

When Saul saw the Philistine army, he was afraid; terror filled his heart.
He inquired of the LORD, but the LORD did not answer him by dreams
or Urim or prophets. Saul then said to his attendants, "Find me a
woman who is a medium, so I may go and inquire of her."
1 SAMUEL 28:5–7 NIV

In his last days, Saul had become increasingly separated from the Lord. He knew it and it upset him. In his madness, he sought God by doing something God was sure to disapprove of. He sought out a witch.

Jewish law specifically forbade witches from living among the people of God, and in more faithful days, Saul had banished them from the country. In a desperate attempt to be reassured he was still doing the right thing, he decided to raise the spirit of the high priest Samuel from the dead.

A medium who could do this was found in Endor, known historically as a difficult place for the laws of Israel to be enforced.

The witch never seemed to feel she was doing wrong even though she was well aware it would be dangerous to be caught doing it. She warned Saul that what he was asking was illegal; she worked her dark arts, and afterward she showed concern for his health and baked bread to feed him. Her identity as a witch seemed firmly fixed in her own mind and caused her little personal concern. But she heard the word of God as

> *Dear Lord, the temptation to do wrong in Your eyes in order to save what we have in this world can sometimes be overpowering. Let us instead be overpowered by You, knowing that even if we lose everything, we gain beyond all expectation if we only stand on Your Word.*

Samuel spoke it against Saul, and she would have heard of Saul's death the next day. Hopefully, she reconsidered her own position as one whom God had spoken against.

Perhaps the real evil in this story goes back to the source of all evil. Saul wanted to be right. He also wanted God on his side. But the two things weren't compatible. Instead of taking time for contemplation, instead of adjusting his position to one that was more in agreement with God's wishes, he went to extreme lengths in the hope of getting God to agree with him. That kind of madness is inspired by the devil. It plays on our need for God and can only end in death.

The same voice that convinced Saul it was okay to seek out one whom God forbade would also have convinced the witch that her skills did not meddle in God's domain and were perfectly acceptable.

There is only one voice worth listening to and it's not the one that contradicts scripture. Saul died for listening to the other voice. We can only hope his example was not lost on the witch of Endor.

CAIN'S WIFE—
Redeemer or Co-Conspirator?

*And Cain went out from the presence of the LORD, and dwelt in
the land of Nod, on the east of Eden. And Cain knew his wife;
and she conceived, and bare Enoch: and he builded a city,
and called the name of the city, after the name of his son, Enoch.*
GENESIS 4:16–17 KJV

The wife of Cain remains forever in the shadow of her husband's violent act—the first murder. So, we can only wonder about her.

The Bible doesn't tell us whether Cain married her before or after his banishment. The timing would be significant. If she married him before he killed his brother, she may have contributed to the bitterness that distanced him from God. If she married him afterward, she must have had a very big heart indeed.

We are not told what it was that God disapproved of in Cain's offering. But it is likely the offering reflected the attitude with which he offered it. Had someone—his wife perhaps—been filling his head with notions of unworthiness? Was she a woman for whom her man could never do enough? Did she think she deserved better? Does that sound at all familiar as you look around today?

The rest of the story—God's disapproval, Abel's death, his parents' grief, and Cain's exile—show just how

> *Father, when Cain killed the firstborn of Your Creation You did not strike him down as would have seemed fair. You sent him away from the people he hurt and provided a wife, a child, and a home. From the beginning of time Your mercy has been beyond comprehension. Take our hand and guide us gently through our losses and pains, teaching us how to respond in love. Perhaps then we might do the same for others.*

insidious and damaging such ingratitude can be.

On the other hand, she may have married him after the infamous event. That would have taken a very special woman indeed. But wouldn't it be just like God to provide a means of redemption even to one who had committed such a terrible crime? Perhaps Cain's wife was chosen as a subtle way to work on his heart, to turn him back toward his Creator.

Does the Bible offer us any clues? Only the one. Cursed to wander the earth, Cain seems to have defied—or been forgiven—that instruction and settled down instead. He and his wife had a son they called Enoch. Cain founded a city, which he named after his son.

What does Enoch mean? It means "dedicated." Could it be that Cain repented of the anger in his heart? Did he regret slaying his brother? Did he dedicate his firstborn son and the world's first city to the God he'd wronged so grievously?

What would cause such a thing to happen? Man, being a stubborn creature, might defy an all-powerful God yet be more amenable to a woman who loves him and sees beyond his obvious flaws.

THE WISE WOMAN OF TEKOA—
Teaching the King His Own Lesson

Then the woman said, "Let your servant speak a word to my lord the king."
"Speak," he replied. The woman said, "Why then have you devised a thing
like this against the people of God? When the king says this, does he
not convict himself, for the king has not brought back his banished son?
Like water spilled on the ground, which cannot be recovered, so we
must die. But that is not what God desires; rather, he devises ways
so that a banished person does not remain banished from him."

2 SAMUEL 14:12–14 NIV

King David, perhaps because of the chaotic nature of his family, found himself in a situation echoing that of Adam. One of his sons had killed the other. Absalom killed Amnon after Amnon raped Absalom's sister.

As the king was grieving his dead son, the living one ran into exile, doubling the loss.

The unnamed wise woman from Tekoa arrived at court and gave quite a performance. Dressed in rags, she threw herself down in front of the king and told a tale of woe wherein one of her sons had killed the other. The people, she said, now wanted to kill her remaining son. If the king allowed it to happen, she would be left destitute and would surely die.

Actually, what she did was recount the tale of Cain and Abel, down to

Grief scares us, Lord. It leaves us feeling impotent and unable to help. This, in turn, leaves the grieving feeling even more isolated. You, though, have provided the teachings that can prevent such loss and pain from becoming a downward, self-perpetuating spiral. Give us the awareness to see that and the courage to take Your words to where they will do the greatest good.

the details of the murder taking place in a field and Cain needing protection from God so he wouldn't be killed in revenge.

She was acting under the instruction of Joab, the commander of David's army, but she was taking a considerable personal risk. Lying to the king, especially in his time of grief, could have had serious consequences. She must have thought the chance worth taking. And she probably didn't think she was lying. In her mind, she may well have simply been recounting the age-old tale of God's mercy in a situation where human instincts cry out for revenge.

David saw through her ploy. The message got through partly in that he called Absalom back from exile. Sadly, he couldn't go all the way and welcome his son back into his presence. The distance he left between them would only grow, with disastrous consequences.

We know nothing more about the wise woman of Tekoa, but we do know she sets an example worth following. God's mercy is often most needed where the pain is greatest. It takes a wise man or woman to realize that—and a brave soul to actually take it there.

THE WIFE FROM BAHURIM—
Afraid but Faithful

*Nevertheless a lad saw them, and told Absalom: but they went both of them
away quickly, and came to a man's house in Bahurim, which had a well in his
court; whither they went down. And the woman took and spread a covering over
the well's mouth, and spread ground corn thereon; and the thing was not known.*
2 SAMUEL 17:18–19 KJV

The plan involved a beleaguered king, a rebellious prince, their
advisers, the Creator of the universe. . .and a housewife whose name
no one remembers!

Absalom was attempting to unite the forces of Israel against his
father, King David. Both men were desperate for advice, but it was
David who took the step of asking God for help. He prayed that
Absalom's advisers would appear foolish. Then, at the summit of the
Mount of Olives, the man who could confound those advisers turned
up, dusty and in rags.

> *Dear Lord, we forget at times just
> how important we are in Your
> eyes and how much You value
> our decisions to do the right thing
> in situations the world might
> consider completely unimportant
> or pointless. Help us to understand
> that choosing between what's right
> or wrong is never an unimportant
> decision, no matter how
> inconsequential it might seem at
> the time.*

Hushai the Arkite
was sent to the court of
Absalom to give advice
that suited David. Having
convinced Absalom to
take a course of action
that would actually benefit
David, he sent word of the
new plan via Jonathan and
Ahimaaz, the sons of loyal
priests.

These two brave men
were observed heading for
David's camp and had to

hide at a town called Bahurim.

The owner of the house might not have been around, or it might have been safer to have his wife act in his place. Regardless, the woman hid Jonathan and Ahimaaz in their family well, covering it up and disguising it so well that it looked like solid ground. Then, when she was confronted by Absalom's angry men, she misdirected them.

The message got through and the story continued with the major players taking center stage once more. But God's plan for King David might have come to an abrupt halt if one woman, with no knowledge of the larger drama being played out, had not decided to do the right thing. At a time when the usurper was in the ascendency, at a time when she had no one around to defend her if she was discovered, she stayed loyal to God's anointed king. She made a bigger difference than she could possibly have known, and then she went on about her everyday life.

Little acts of courage, loyalty, and honesty play a larger part in God's plans than any of us imagine. When you are challenged on your beliefs, on your honor, on what you believe to be right, remember the courage of the wife from Bahurim. Stand up for the good and know you also are playing your part in a greater battle.

MANOAH'S WIFE—
A Chosen Woman

The angel of the LORD appeared to her and said, "You are barren and childless, but you are going to become pregnant and give birth to a son. Now see to it that you drink no wine or other fermented drink and that you do not eat anything unclean. You will become pregnant and have a son whose head is never to be touched by a razor because the boy is to be a Nazirite, dedicated to God from the womb. He will take the lead in delivering Israel from the hands of the Philistines."

JUDGES 13:3–5 NIV

Samson is the dominant figure in his life story, but his mother and father also have a tale to tell. As a couple with no children, they undoubtedly suffered some stigma in a society where the number of children you had usually reflected your wealth and standing in society.

But then Manoah's wife, Samson's mother, was visited by an angel. She became part of that chosen group of women whose child was foretold by heaven.

Interestingly, despite the fact that her husband is named and she isn't, the angel of the Lord was more interested in her than in him. He conveyed the message and God's instructions directly to her. She told her husband, and Manoah petitioned God for another visitation. When the angel returned, he appeared again before the wife rather than the husband.

When Manoah questioned the angel, he simply repeated what he told Manoah's wife. When Manoah tried to entice

> *The need to understand runs deep in many of us, Lord, and it is generally a useful trait in this life. Forgive us, Lord, when we forget that You are beyond and above this world and will not be understood unless You make it so. Trust and obedience are what we need. Understanding will surely come later.*

him to stay—perhaps to show him off—the angel showed him how foolish he was being.

In the end, Manoah and his wife fell flat on the ground in awe and fear. But it was Manoah who was fearful, not her. Manoah needed to be reassured by his wife that they would not die as a result of the visitations.

The question has to be asked—how would we react in a similar situation? Manoah wanted more; he wanted to dictate terms, ask questions, and possibly impress his neighbors. Those responses might have played a part in him expecting to incur God's wrath.

Manoah's wife, on the other hand, was shocked but listened respectfully. She shared what had happened with her husband, obeyed the angel's instructions, and accepted the whole thing as a wonderful gift from above. She knew they weren't about to die because through their son, God had promised them a future.

God always wants the best for us, but we have to play our part. And if we are faithful, everything that comes from God will be a gift.

THE WOMAN ON THE TOWER AT THEBEZ—
Fighting for Love

But there was a strong tower within the city, and thither fled all the men and women, and all they of the city, and shut it to them, and gat them up to the top of the tower. And Abimelech came unto the tower, and fought against it, and went hard unto the door of the tower to burn it with fire. And a certain woman cast a piece of a millstone upon Abimelech's head, and all to brake his skull.

JUDGES 9:51–53 KJV

In the time of the judges, the Israelites believed they ought to be ruled by God or His chosen priest or judge. Gideon, the last of the judges, reiterated the claim that the people of God ought only to be ruled by God. But he didn't always live up to his own ideals.

His son Abimelech went even further astray, claiming the kingship for himself and killing seventy brothers in the process. If his father had initially been unsure of his calling, Abimelech was certain of his to the point of megalomania. No one was allowed to stand in his way. Cities were besieged, civilian populations were slaughtered.

For a while, it looked like his all-consuming conceit might carry him all the way to the throne. But God has a habit of using the humble to bring the mighty down.

During the battle for the city of Thebez, the people retreated to a strong tower to make their last stand. Abimelech, doubtless thinking he was invincible, personally approached the entrance to

> *Dear Lord, spare us from the conceit in our minds that places ourselves above Your other children, our brothers and sisters. If You would have us make a mark on this world, let it not be through the drive for personal success. Rather, let it be anonymous and on the side of love.*

the tower to set it alight. His intention was to burn everyone inside.

But a nameless woman on the roof of the tower had other ideas. Large rocks and stone would have been taken to the top of the tower to be used as weapons. Risking her own safety (and perhaps driven by the desire to save her family), this woman carried a broken millstone to the edge of the roof and threw it at the king.

Despite being struck a mortal blow, Abimelech's pride ruled him to the end. He insisted that one of his own men run him through with a sword so no one could say the great king was killed by a woman.

Pride in yourself: God's not a big fan of it. He will always judge it harshly, often using "little" people acting in love to bring it down. The woman on the tower at Thebez never had her name recorded and may never have made another impression on history. But she freed Israel from a tyrant king, giving it yet another chance to turn to God.

JEPHTHAH'S DAUGHTER—
A Good Sacrifice or a Bad Bargain?

When Jephthah returned to his home in Mizpah, who should come out to meet him but his daughter, dancing to the sound of timbrels! She was an only child. Except for her he had neither son nor daughter. When he saw her, he tore his clothes and cried, "Oh no, my daughter! You have brought me down and I am devastated. I have made a vow to the LORD that I cannot break."

JUDGES 11:34–35 NIV

The story of Jephthah's daughter is a controversial one.

Jephthah, the son of Gilead and a prostitute, is driven from his home by jealous family members. Despite this (or perhaps because of it), he became a mighty warrior and his people called him back again when they needed his prowess in war. Still loyal but wary because of their past behavior, he negotiated a permanent role as their leader on the condition that he was successful in battle.

The pressure was really on. This was his big chance to show them what he was worth. To ensure success, he made a deal with God, promising the Creator a sacrifice—the first thing to greet him from his own home when he returned from his victory. Perhaps he expected his dog to greet him. Perhaps there was a servant he wasn't overly fond of. Instead his only daughter came, singing and dancing, to meet him.

> Almighty God, we are ungrateful indeed when we try to bargain with You for more than the plenty You have already provided. Help us to look within our hearts, within our own homes, and within Your Word for all that we might need and trust that we will find it. May our prayers be praise and thanks instead of deals and bargains where others might have to pay the price.

When her heartbroken father told her he must sacrifice her life, she agreed, asking only for two months grace to roam the hills and weep with her friends because she would never marry. Scripture suggests that this began an annual tradition where young unmarried girls "go out" for four days to celebrate the memory of Jephthah's daughter.

Despite the example shown in the story of Abraham and Isaac, and the fact that human sacrifice was never an acceptable way to worship Jehovah (in fact, it was often the standard by which He condemned idolatrous peoples), Jephthah fulfills his vow.

Bible scholars (and Jewish rabbis) have long argued over the meaning and best interpretation of this tragic story.

She was never named in the Bible, but the story of Jephthah's daughter is nonetheless a powerful one. To many, she remains a symbol of purity—a daughter willing to do the bidding of her father on earth and her Father in heaven no matter what the personal cost. To others, she is an example of how foolish it is to think you can do a deal with God by offering anything other than yourself—and to offer it so completely.

THE MOTHER OF RUFUS—
Mother to the Children of Christ

Greet Rufus, chosen in the Lord, and his mother,
who has been a mother to me, too.
ROMANS 16:13 NIV

Many of the women in the Bible are named simply "Mother of. . . ,"
"Daughter of. . . ," or "Wife of. . ." Rufus's mother falls into that cate-
gory, but we can speculate a little more in her case than is the usual.

It's generally thought that Rufus, whom Paul salutes in his epi-
stle to the Romans, is the son of Simon the Cyrene—the man who
helped carry Christ's cross on the long walk to Calvary. A Jew from
Cyrene (in Libya), Simon may have been on a pilgrimage to the
temple in Jerusalem. His wife may well have been beside him at the
fateful moment when he carried Christ's burden. That their son would
later become a pillar of the church speaks to the effect the encounter with Jesus may have had on them personally.

> Lord, help us remember that
> You are Father to us all and the
> love we show to Your sons and
> daughters is love shown to You.
> Take away the worldly barriers
> that separate us from each other,
> and help us to see that anything
> that keeps the children of God
> apart can only be the work of the
> enemy. May we ask, like Your Son
> did, "Who is My mother? Who are
> My brothers?" And may we find we
> have family of all kinds among
> the children of God.

Rufus is mentioned as being "chosen in the Lord," and his mother is mentioned in the same sentence. There can be no doubt that both mother and son were strong in the faith, perhaps holding important positions in the church in Rome. But not only did Rufus's mother raise a godly son, she also appears to have supported the apostle Paul in some of his many times of trial, treating him as she would her own son. While other members of Paul's family are mentioned in the Bible, we hear nothing about his natural mother. Even if she still lived, she would have played no part in his ministry. To the apostle, who was often under attack far from home, the maternal love offered by Rufus's mother must have been especially comforting.

We can draw a bigger lesson from her behavior, one that applies to each of us. To Rufus's mother, a young male Christian was a son whether he was physically related to her or not. Doubtless younger women in the faith were daughters to her and elders were respected as parents. If we would truly be a family under God, we need to see each other as more than people who simply share the same faith. We need to see them as real brothers, sisters, fathers, and mothers. We need to love our spiritual family as we would biological family. Imagine how that would make our heavenly Father smile.

PAUL'S SISTER—
Mother to Courage

But when the son of Paul's sister heard of this plot, he went into the barracks and told Paul. Then Paul called one of the centurions and said, "Take this young man to the commander; he has something to tell him." So he took him to the commander.

ACTS 23:16–18 NIV

⁂

The apostle Paul is such a dominant figure in the New Testament that it is hard to imagine he sprang from an ordinary family. An only child would have been a rare thing in times when large families were prized and respected. He may have had many brothers and sisters, but the Bible only mentions one of his siblings—his unnamed sister.

Like Paul, his sister was most likely a native of the Jewish community in Tarsus (in Turkey). Their family seems to have been at least moderately well off. They were Roman citizens during a time when citizenship was a highly prized mark of status. They could afford to send at least one son, Paul, to study in Jerusalem under the best Jewish teachers of the time. What his sister was doing in the same city later (if indeed she was there) is left unexplained.

Father of us all, we are reminded that Your plans to help us are laid in place long before our times of need arise. When they come upon us, we need to understand that it is either Your will that we be there or that someone—a relative or a stranger—will already have laid the groundwork for our rescue, whether they are aware of it or not!

The first mention of his sister comes when Paul has returned to Jerusalem after long and arduous travels. She may conceivably have been traveling with him, but as the mother of a son her place would have been with her family, either in Tarsus or Jerusalem. Her son, Paul's nephew, was definitely in Jerusalem at the time his uncle was mobbed and arrested. It is possible that Paul's parents were also there.

Paul's father was a Pharisee of note, so we might assume it was a considerable shock to see his son throw his training aside to champion this new "sect." In a world where daughters were more easily controlled, it is unlikely that Paul's sister followed him into Christianity (at least openly). She would probably have been married to a man of similar stature and inclination to her father. Perhaps her husband was also a Pharisee and his temple obligations brought them to Jerusalem. Or perhaps their son was following in his grand-father's footsteps.

The only other thing we know for sure about the sister of Paul is that she raised a courageous son who was either a lover of justice or a fan of his uncle Paul (or perhaps both). The apostle Paul, and all of Christianity, would have good reason to thank her for that alone.

So, the influence of a mother (and sister) can spread far beyond her own life.

PAUL'S NEPHEW—
A Rebel in the Cause of Right

Then the chief captain took him by the hand, and went with him aside privately,
and asked him, What is that thou hast to tell me? And he said, The Jews have
agreed to desire thee that thou wouldest bring down Paul to morrow into the
council, as though they would enquire somewhat of him more perfectly. But do not
thou yield unto them: for there lie in wait for him of them more than forty men,
which have bound themselves with an oath, that they will neither eat nor drink
till they have killed him: and now are they ready, looking for a promise from thee.
ACTS 23:19–21 KJV

Paul was a radical. He was preaching that Judaism, the faith of his own people, had been superseded by Christianity. Understandably, there were elements of Jewish society who didn't appreciate this. Given that he came from a family of Pharisees, there may have been members of his own family who didn't agree with his message.

Some took it too far, though. After a riot in the temple left Paul imprisoned, forty Jewish men banded together and decided to kill him for his "blasphemy." These men weren't shy, and they must have been men of influence because they told the priests and elders about their plan. The priests and elders seemed to be in agreement with them.

Either through chance or because he was in some way connected to one of the priests and elders (or

Almighty God, in a world that values power and influence, help us not to sell ourselves in pursuit of those false gods. Should we hear of some wrongdoing, give us the heart to speak against it, valuing right and love far above earthly favor. After all, our position in this world is transitory and tarnished if it is not Your will, but our position in Your kingdom will be glorious and eternal.

perhaps to one of the forty men), Paul's nephew heard of the plot and decided to risk his own life thwarting it.

Make no mistake, if these men had sworn not to eat or drink until they killed Paul, they would also surely kill anyone who tried to save him.

The unnamed nephew took word of the plot to the commander of the Roman barracks where Paul was being held. Such was the danger that the commander immediately sent Paul away from Jerusalem under the guard of "two hundred soldiers, seventy horsemen and two hundred spearmen" (Acts 23:23 NIV). He also urged Paul's nephew not to speak of what had happened, no doubt for his own safety.

We can't tell whether Paul's nephew considered himself a Jew or a Christian, but we can be certain the young man had a strong sense of right and wrong and was prepared to risk his life for what was right. A family trait, perhaps, that Paul would carry to its ultimate conclusion when he died for the Way, the Truth, and the Life.

SISERA'S MOTHER—
Waiting for Her Share

"Through the window peered Sisera's mother; behind the lattice she cried out,
'Why is his chariot so long in coming? Why is the clatter of his chariots delayed?'
The wisest of her ladies answer her; indeed, she keeps saying to herself,
'Are they not finding and dividing the spoils: a woman or two for each man,
colorful garments as plunder for Sisera, colorful garments embroidered,
highly embroidered garments for my neck—all this as plunder?'"
JUDGES 5:28–30 NIV

Soldiers are sometimes called on to do terrible things. But, like the rest of us, they can choose to do what they are commanded righteously or otherwise. As a servant of an occupying king, Sisera was a very effective commander of the army, but he was known more for his cruel oppression than his justice and mercy.

When God decided this occupation should end, He instructed His prophetess Deborah on how to bring it about. Fighting under God's instruction, the army of Israel routed Sisera's forces. While his army fled on their chariots, Sisera took the cowardly option, running away on his own, hoping the Israelites would not find him. He took refuge in the tent of a man whose family had an alliance with his king and hid there.

Wonderful Father, raising children is difficult. It has the potential to be one of the greatest or one of the saddest things we will ever do in this life. What will make the difference is whether we choose to fill our children's hearts with our desires or with Your love.

In times of frustration and impatience, remind us that we are not only raising a child of our own, but also a beloved child of the Most High King.

Unfortunately for him, the woman of the house was loyal to Israel and she killed him while he slept.

Afterward, Deborah sang a song about the victory, taking the time to imagine how Sisera's mother would feel. She was sure Sisera's mother would assume he had won the battle and would even then be dividing up the spoils of war, including a couple of women for each of the victorious men.

Doubtless, in real life Sisera's mother would be distraught when she heard of his death. But the question would have to be asked—what role did she play in raising this warrior, known for his cruelty but willing to abandon his army in defeat?

Despite being seen as powerless in patriarchal society, mothers everywhere exercise a lot of power in the way they raise their children. A boy's idea of the man he should be will be heavily influenced by his mother's idea of what a man should be.

Raising an honorable, God-fearing son will not necessarily keep him safe in whatever battles he has to fight, but it could assure his place in heaven and make sure his memory on the earth is one of love and respect rather than infamy and disgrace.

THE WISE WOMAN OF ABEL—
Speaking Peace in Wartime

And when he was come near unto her, the woman said, Art thou Joab?
And he answered, I am he. Then she said unto him, Hear the words of thine
handmaid. And he answered, I do hear. Then she spake, saying, They were
wont to speak in old time, saying, They shall surely ask counsel at Abel: and so
they ended the matter. I am one of them that are peaceable and faithful in Israel:
thou seekest to destroy a city and a mother in Israel: why wilt thou swallow
up the inheritance of the LORD? And Joab answered and said, Far be it,
far be it from me, that I should swallow up or destroy.
2 SAMUEL 20:17–20 KJV

When men get up a head of steam they can be difficult to stop. The mix of aggression and pride often leaves nothing but devastation in its wake. Women are often the ones left to make the best of what remains, but sometimes, if they are wise and brave, they can halt the conflict before it begins.

In the time following King David's battles with his son Absalom, there were many divisions in the ranks of the army and the tribes of Israel. One man who spoke against David was called Sheba, son of Bikri.

Sheba took himself to the heartland of those who might oppose the king and found refuge in the city of Abel. Unfortunately for him, his pursuer was Joab, a ruthless commander of the forces loyal to David. He and his men were determined to kill Sheba, even if it meant destroying the ancient city

> *Almighty God, Your voice is ever present for those willing to hear it. May we either be willing servants braving personal peril to voice those words when the world needs to hear them, or may we have a heart to hear the words and realize they come from You.*

of Abel to get him.

The defenders and the attackers were set up for an epic battle when one woman stepped forward. She challenged Joab to think about the destruction he would wreak. The city of Abel, she reminded him, was honored in Israel's history as a city of wisdom. Did he want to be the one who destroyed such a gem?

It must have taken courage to defy such a famous soldier. It must also have taken courage to turn to her own people, supporters of Sheba, and say that one man's death would mean life for many more. They agreed. Sheba's head was thrown out of the city. Content, Joab withdrew. The city of Abel remained intact, as did the many families living within its walls.

When men's strength and determination goes unchecked, they will often be their own worst enemies. Women who bravely speak wisdom to them are usually best placed to save the men from themselves. And God is to be praised for organizing things so.

PILATE'S WIFE—
A Voice of God in a
Court of Power

When he was set down on the judgment seat, his wife sent unto him,
saying, Have thou nothing to do with that just man: for I have
suffered many things this day in a dream because of him.
MATTHEW 27:19 KJV

As a man of earthly power, Pontius Pilate was also a man at the mercy of earthly power. In the political games going on at the time, the Roman governor seemed to have been well played by the Jewish priests. He found himself judging a man he believed to be innocent, but priestly machinations and the maintenance of his position seemed to demand that Pilate execute him.

But even when a person surrounds himself with earthly power and influence, he is not beyond the reach of heaven. In this instance, God talked to Pilate through the conscience (or the dreams) of his unnamed wife. In strong terms she urged Pilate to believe that Jesus was a just man and to walk away from the possibility of passing judgment on Him. Despite her privileged position as his

> *Dear Lord, even those who might be seen as enemies of the faith will do Your bidding if You require it of them. How much more should we serve since we profess faith! Keep us open to Your instructions in whatever way You deem it best to send them. May we search always for Your Word, awake or asleep, at rest or at work. Then grant us the courage to be the instruments by which Your Word changes this world. We may never know the impact a God-inspired dream might have, and so we act in faith, trusting You to provide a wonderful conclusion.*

wife, it must have taken considerable courage for her to interrupt the governor at such an important time. She actually went further than that—she asked him to show weakness, something men of earthly power are rarely strong enough to do.

Legend and tradition say that Pilate's wife was influenced by Jewish teaching. As such, she would have been familiar with the texts predicting a messiah and the threat such a man represented to the ruling regime of the day. But her knowledge of Jesus as a just man, a man worth taking such a risk for, could only have come to her from God. Several Eastern traditions have her converting to and working for Christianity later in her life. There may be no truth in these legends, but her inclusion in the biblical account shows her as a woman profoundly (and surprisingly) affected by the presence of Jesus, so the possibility of her converting to Christianity should not be discounted.

If nothing else—and this is surely something of great worth— the story of Pilate's wife shows there is no place—be it the lion's den, captivity in Egypt, or in a court bristling with military power—where God cannot make His presence felt if He so desires.

THE WOMEN AT CALVARY—
The Mothers of His Ministry

Many women were there, watching from a distance. They had followed Jesus
from Galilee to care for his needs. Among them were Mary Magdalene,
Mary the mother of James and Joseph, and the mother of Zebedee's sons.
MATTHEW 27:55–56 NIV

⁕

Perhaps one of the most difficult things you can do for someone is
share in their suffering when there is nothing you can do to allevi-
ate it.

Talking of the crucifixion, Matthew mentions "many women"
who watched Jesus die. Some of them are mentioned by name in the
Gospels. Mary, the mother of Jesus, Mary the wife of Clopas, and
Mary Magdalene are mentioned as having been there, but who were
the others?

They were lovers of the Lord. That much is certain. They could
have hidden away, protesting that this was all too much for them, but
instead they attended His agony and wept with Him through His
greatest earthly trial. They publicly declared themselves as followers
of a "dangerous" man when the men of influence who had insisted on His death were also present. They were brave.

But they were also an essential part of His ministry. The apostle Paul supported himself by working as a tent maker during his travels. But Jesus dedicated Himself completely to proclaiming

> *Heavenly Father, keep us always aware that You build Your kingdom on foundations of humble service. May we not look down on those who garner no public acclaim through their work for You. Indeed, may we emulate their hearts and become such servants, knowing we will be closer to You in that role than in any other.*

the kingdom of God. He trusted wholly in God's provision. His disciples were similarly employed—and unemployed. They were fishermen who didn't fish, tax collectors who collected no coins, and so on.

Which is where the unnamed women came in. As supporters of Jesus' ministry and followers of His, they needed to have the freedom to travel, which suggests they were most likely widows or older unmarried women. They most likely had some disposable income that they were willing to spend in pursuance of God's work. After the death of Jesus, they could have quietly returned home—but then came the resurrection. The mission still on, these women probably continued supporting the disciples, perhaps even playing important roles in the fledgling church.

And yet, they are hardly known or acknowledged by history or popular memory. Ironically, such devout humble service—not done for personal gain or recognition—is usually seen as the mark of a true Christian.

They did what they did out of love for Jesus. Their efforts would have cost them time, money, perhaps social status and marital or family prospects—but the rewards implicit in His love would have outweighed all of that. They enabled the earthly ministry of Jesus and stayed with Him as He brought that mission to its heartbreaking conclusion. Then they helped ensure the message lived on.

Their places in heaven were most certainly assured.

THE SERVANT OF
NAAMAN'S WIFE—
A Servant of God First

Now bands of raiders from Aram had gone out and had taken captive a young girl
from Israel, and she served Naaman's wife. She said to her mistress, "If only my
master would see the prophet who is in Samaria! He would cure him of his leprosy."

2 KINGS 5:2–3 NIV

Imagine a young woman: living her life, helping with the family chores, perhaps wondering about marriage and children in the future. Now imagine her kidnapped, taken to a foreign land, and made to serve the family of a high-ranking soldier. All her dreams for the future have just been shattered. She would have every right to be bitter, every right to hate her captors and have no reason to love them—except that her God expected her to.

The head of the family she served was Naaman, a soldier highly regarded by the king of Aram. Naaman had everything going for him—position, power, the ear of the king—and then he contracted leprosy!

In those days, leprosy was seen as a curse from God and people with it were often shunned or cast out. All the unnamed serving girl had to do was to wait for the illness to progress—wait for her master's house to, metaphorically, fall down around him.

But she didn't. She saw

> *Dear Lord above, Your will is that we should be instruments of Your grace and all else is secondary. Should Your plans not match our expectations, help us appreciate that You have plans and intentions we cannot imagine. May our focus be always on serving You and bringing others to You, leaving our future and everything else in Your more than capable hands.*

a man who was suffering and she knew a prophet, Elisha, who could help. Elisha lived in her homeland of Israel, so she told her mistress about him, and she told her husband. Namaan was given permission by the king to go and seek a cure.

The serving girl didn't ask to go with him although she must have longed to see her homeland again. In fact, she doesn't seem to have asked anything for herself. Neither is there any record that she was rewarded for her efforts. But she did it anyway.

She saw someone suffering and—as Jesus often did when He looked out on the people following Him—she took pity on him. She put her own situation and difficulties to one side and directed a sufferer to God, the ultimate healer.

She would not have known that the story of what happened next would be told for centuries, or that she would hardly be noticed in that story, lost in the shadows of a king, a great commander, and one of the greatest prophets. Given what we know about this young woman, we might surmise that playing a small part in spreading the story of God's mercy would have been enough for her, warming her soul despite her personal situation.

LOT'S WIFE—
Just What Was She Looking For?

Most of the people in the Bible stories are known for how they lived their lives, whether good or bad, faithful or faithless. The wife of Lot is remembered almost exclusively for the manner of her death.

She is generally assumed to be a native of the city of Sodom, which, now as then, was no great recommendation as to her virtue. When God decided to destroy the city for its sins, He said He would spare it if ten righteous men could be found in the city. In the end, only one righteous man could be found—Lot! As the wife of the only man in the city worth saving, we might assume he had some influence over her. Hopefully, his wife was a godly woman. If she wasn't, she was about to see Lot's faith affirmed by a mighty work of God.

> Our Father, the voices and distractions of this world are many and seductive. Clear our minds that we might see them for the deceptions—the works of the enemy—that they really are. Help us to listen to and desire only that which is pure and honest and loving—and of You!

We know that Lot was a man of some influence in the city (although if he had had more influence the city might have been spared). But we can surmise that, as the wife of a wealthy man, Lot's wife had a comfortable life, a nice house, all her needs met.

The angels sent to save the family actually had to take them by the hand and pull them toward safety. Perhaps they didn't really believe the city would be destroyed. Perhaps they were reluctant to abandon their comfortable lives.

The angels took them a safe distance away, warning them not to look back. We can only speculate as to what Lot's wife was missing when she did look back—family, friends, position, fine clothes, an elegant home...the things that divert many from lives of faith.

God had a future in mind for Lot's family, but she couldn't let go of the past, insisting on looking backward rather than forward. And she turned into a pillar of salt, completely dehydrated, perhaps by the intensity of a blast that destroyed a city obsessed by greed and self-gratification.

If she teaches us anything, Lot's wife shows us the futility of being too attached to earthly things. These are temporary and God given. When He removes them from us, as He is entitled to do, we should look ahead to the newer and better life He has arranged for us.

THE MAN BORN BLIND—
He Saw Jesus for Who He Really Was

Then they hurled insults at him and said, "You are this fellow's disciple!
We are disciples of Moses! We know that God spoke to Moses, but as for this
fellow, we don't even know where he comes from." The man answered,
"Now that is remarkable! You don't know where he comes from, yet he opened
my eyes. We know that God does not listen to sinners. He listens to the godly
person who does his will. Nobody has ever heard of opening the eyes of a
man born blind. If this man were not from God, he could do nothing."

JOHN 9:28–33 NIV

⸺⸺⸺

Jesus' disciples assumed that either the man or his parents had sinned, resulting in his blindness. An old-fashioned belief, but one that is still prevalent today. People often make assumptions of blame or sinful behavior when they see others suffering. These assumptions often provide the excuse needed not to help.

Jesus pointed out that the man's condition had nothing to do with sin; it was meant for the glory of God's love. Then He restored the man's eyes.

When we see people in troubled situations, we might not be able to heal their disabilities, but by showing them love, by offering a helping hand, we, too, are glorifying God.

> Lord, You have done so much for me, even to the beating of my heart, the working of my mind, and the sight of my eyes. I am a miracle only because I am a work of Yours. May I proclaim it always!

The man born blind was almost immediately thrust into a difficult situation. He didn't see who healed him, but the Pharisees demanded he identify the man so they could condemn him for "working" on the Sabbath. The man simply stated that someone healed him, and no one who was "in sin" could have performed such a miracle.

It's a measure of how much courage it took to defy the Pharisees when even his parents, who must have been stunned to see their son healed, were almost too scared to confirm what had happened to him.

Gradually, the man who was born blind figures the situation out for himself, even going so far as to mock the Pharisees for their inability to see the obvious. For a man who must have spent his life depending on others, this is an amazing transformation.

When he meets Jesus again, seeing Him for the first time, he says, "Lord, I believe."

We might think that no one could deny a miracle or the power behind it. But the Pharisees were apparently prepared to. People throughout the centuries since then have lived in a world full of miracles and wonders without ever looking properly at the everyday miracles that surround them.

Be one of those who really see. Look around at God's creation and, like the man who was born blind (but didn't stay that way), say, "Lord, I believe!"

THE WOMAN OF SAMARIA—
Jesus Breaks the Rules

The woman saith unto him, I know that Messias cometh, which is called Christ:
when he is come, he will tell us all things. Jesus saith unto her, I that speak unto
thee am he. And upon this came his disciples, and marvelled that he talked with
the woman: yet no man said, What seekest thou? or, Why talkest thou with her?
The woman then left her waterpot, and went her way into the city, and saith to the
men, Come, see a man, which told me all things that ever I did: is not this the Christ?
JOHN 4:25–29 KJV

Jesus really shouldn't have talked to her—but it almost seems as if she were the sole reason for His journey.

John mentions that Jesus had to travel through Samaria, suggesting it was not a thing most Jews did willingly. There was a historic antagonism between the Samaritans and the Jews, with both sides declaring the other spiritually unclean.

Approaching Jacob's Well, Jesus sent His disciples on ahead. Why? Did He perhaps have another preordained appointment?

When the Samaritan woman approached, He asked her for a drink of water. She immediately understood that this was wrong. Jews and Samaritans did not associate with each other. Plus, she was an unaccompanied woman. Propriety demanded that Jesus, as a rabbi, should not be seen talking to her. Thereafter Jesus began discussing spiritual matters with her, which was also forbidden. He revealed that He knew she was a woman living in sin.

> *Wonderful Jesus, in the depths of*
> *our despair, in our shame, in the*
> *aftermath of our own wrongdoing,*
> *it is a wonderful feeling beyond*
> *all understanding that You will*
> *be there for us with the gift of*
> *everlasting life. And all we have*
> *to do is ask—and receive!*

Given all of those reasons, she was perhaps the last person Jesus should have been speaking to. Then He did another incredible thing. He revealed Himself as the Messiah to her, something He almost never did.

The woman declared His presence to the Samaritans, and many came to faith through her. Jesus seemed to predict her future—and that of the faith—saying there would come a time when she would worship neither on Mount Gerizim (sacred to the Samaritans) or Jerusalem (sacred to the Jews), but she would worship the Father in the Spirit.

Combine those words with the good work she did bringing her townspeople to Jesus, it might also be thought that the Lord was preparing her for life as a missionary. What happened afterward is not recorded in the Bible, but Eastern tradition says this woman brought many to faith.

She was a sinner and spiritually unclean, but she accepted the living waters and her soul was washed clean.

By all the laws of society, Jesus really shouldn't have talked to her, but the law of grace has a habit of taking sinners and transforming them into something wonderful.

THE WIDOW WITH THE
JAR OF OLIVE OIL—
Asked in Faith, Received Abundantly

Elisha said, "Go around and ask all your neighbors for empty jars. Don't ask for just a few. Then go inside and shut the door behind you and your sons. Pour oil into all the jars, and as each is filled, put it to one side." She left him and shut the door behind her and her sons. They brought the jars to her and she kept pouring. When all the jars were full, she said to her son, "Bring me another one." But he replied, "There is not a jar left." Then the oil stopped flowing.

2 KINGS 4:3–6 NIV

⎯⎯⎯⎯ ⚬⚬⚬ ⎯⎯⎯⎯

Being in faith does not mean we don't have to deal with the problems inherent in an ordinary life. This woman was the wife of a prophet who served under the great Elisha. Her husband died, as is the way of all flesh, and she had a difficult time coping without him. She had sons but they were too young to be breadwinners.

Debt collectors were harassing her, threatening to sell her children into slavery if she didn't pay them, but all she had to sell was a single jar of oil.

So, she asked Elisha for help.

He told her to ask her neighbors for empty jars, and not to ask for only a few. Then he had her fill the many jars from the single jar. Every single one was filled, and there was still oil in the original jar. She had enough to pay her debts and

> *Lord, whether we should give away all we have, or the world should take it all from us, we still have You. You are more than able to meet our needs, and in You we find our cup of blessings really does overflow. May we never despair, remembering instead that the God who made the world and all the good things in it loves us and will not forget us in our time of need.*

enough left over to live on.

In helping her, Elisha did two things. First, he predicted Jesus' miracles. The filled jars were reminiscent of the water being turned to wine at Cana, and the constant supply of oil predated the plentiful supply of bread and fish when Jesus would feed the multitudes. He also showed that God supplies abundantly if we only ask in faith.

Luke describes the rewards of giving as "a good measure, pressed down, shaken together and running over, will be poured into your lap. For with the measure you use, it will be measured to you" (Luke 6:38 NIV). This woman certainly seems to have been amply rewarded. It's tempting to think of the miracle as a reward for her husband's good work—a pension of sorts—but it is more likely she was simply a woman of faith asking the Lord's prophet for help, in the full expectation that God would supply what she needed.

He did then; He still does now.

THE WIFE SOLD TO
REPAY A DEBT—
Victim of Another's Sin

"Therefore, the kingdom of heaven is like a king who wanted to settle accounts with his servants. As he began the settlement, a man who owed him ten thousand bags of gold was brought to him. Since he was not able to pay, the master ordered that he and his wife and his children and all that he had be sold to repay the debt."

MATTHEW 18:23–25 NIV

Perhaps Jesus had a specific woman in mind when He told the parable of a man ordered by his master to sell his wife and children in order to pay his debt. It's possible she was simply a fictional creation used to illustrate the parable, but given His nature and the fact that such practices still exist in the world, it is likely He had several women and many children in mind.

In the parable, the king is owed an immense amount of gold by his servant. When the servant cannot repay the debt, the king orders that he and his family be sold. It is doubtful that even several wives and many children would have brought in enough gold to pay the debt. This is the point that Jesus is making. God has given us gifts and blessings beyond any possibility of repayment.

> *"I didn't mean it," is a cry You, Father God, must hear all the time when we hurt others through our neglect. Help us to turn that attitude around. Teach us to "mean it," that is, to live meaningful lives and for the meaning of our lives to be You.*

The king forgives his servant—but then the servant is less forgiving with someone who owes him a lesser amount. The point was that we should give as we have been given. Or, at least, try our best.

In this world, however, debt-holders are generally

less forgiving than God is. Those debts might be financial and owed to banks and moneylenders, but they might also be owed to sinful habits and practices. Addictions of many kinds can be seen as people we have mortgaged our souls to, and the wives and children (or husbands and children) often end up paying the price of the sin.

All too often, people convince themselves that it is all right to sin—to take this pill, to have those drinks, to inject something that will make them feel better. After all, they say, it's only ourselves we are hurting. But the innocent woman sold to pay a debt is a reminder that other people all too often end up bearing the brunt of our indebtedness.

The only way to ensure that they don't is to not sell yourself to sin in the first place.

If you want to attempt to pay God back for all you owe Him, then love the innocent for Him. And the most effective way to do that is by making sure you never place yourself in a position where you might need to "sell" them.

THE WOMAN TAKEN
IN ADULTERY—
Between Heaven and Earth

When they kept on questioning him, he straightened up and said to them,
"Let any one of you who is without sin be the first to throw a stone at her."
Again he stooped down and wrote on the ground. At this, those who heard
began to go away one at a time, the older ones first, until only Jesus was left,
with the woman still standing there. Jesus straightened up and asked her,
"Woman, where are they? Has no one condemned you?"

JOHN 8:7–10 NIV

The woman taken in adultery might be any one of us, standing between the forces of the world and the mercy of heaven.

The Pharisees come out of this confrontation particularly poorly. The way they presented the woman to Jesus suggests they had her imprisoned, waiting to use her as bait in a trap. They presented her—and shamed her—publicly, demanding her death. By not demanding the same punishment for the man she committed adultery with, they showed that they had only condemned the more vulnerable of the pair.

Sitting, listening to their demands that she be stoned, Jesus must have been tempted to despair. Indeed, there is a suggestion that by writing in the dust He literally "wrote them

> *Lord, we know but all too often forget that we are not without sin, but our natural instinct seems to be to condemn. Your example showed us there is nothing natural about that instinct. It is a part of our fallen nature, which is part of the devil's work and only leads to more condemnation and pain. If we would be children of heaven rather than subjects of this world, then let our first instinct be always to forgive, as You have forgiven us.*

off." Jeremiah 17:13 says, "LORD, you are the hope of Israel; all who forsake you will be put to shame. Those who turn away from you will be written in the dust" (NIV). Perhaps, if He did indeed write their names in the dust, He was actually writing their spiritual obituary.

Then He showed them the folly of judgment, suggesting that only those who have never sinned could stone the adulteress for her sin.

That she was guilty was never really in doubt. That each one of us has fallen into sin at one time or another is also not in doubt. Left to the forces of the world—revenge, condemnation, soulless application of laws—none of us would stand a chance if our sins were paraded for the world like this woman's sin was.

In the end, her accusers disappeared and she was left face-to-face with God's mercy. When Jesus told her to go and sin no more, He wasn't doing it for the sake of the law; He did it for her sake.

Her story is a constant reminder that even the worst of us (and the law had condemned her to death, after all) can find a new beginning in God's love and mercy.

HERODIAS'S DAUGHTER—
Dancing with the Devil

But when Herod's birthday was kept, the daughter of Herodias danced before
them, and pleased Herod. Whereupon he promised with an oath to give her
whatsoever she would ask. And she, being before instructed of her mother,
said, Give me here John Baptist's head in a charger. And the king was sorry:
nevertheless for the oath's sake, and them which sat with him at meat,
he commanded it to be given her.

MATTHEW 14:6–9 KJV

⁂

Most people, when asked who demanded the head of John the Baptist in return for her dance will suggest it was Salome. But the only Salome mentioned in the Bible is a follower of Christ. The girl whose dance so excited Herod is referred to as Herodias's daughter or even as sharing the same name as her mother. The notion that her name was Salome comes to us from Jewish tradition and has been reinforced by Hollywood.

Whatever her name was, she was raised in an environment of power and privilege. Many would imagine this to be a good thing, but as a result, her values came to be far from godly. She was prepared to let herself be used, both by her mother for political ends and as sexual entertainment for Herod and the men of the court. The innocent child she once was had been smothered by luxury. The young woman she became valued life so little

> Lord, we might dream of lives of luxury but, for the most part, we should thank You for sparing us from lives where caring and being cared for are easy, where sacrifice isn't needed, and where we never need to be tested or grow. Such "hardships" are merely the pressure of the Potter's fingers, forming us into more worthy vessels for Your love.

that she had a man beheaded on another's whim.

Perhaps unknowingly she silenced the voice that proclaimed her mother's sin and the sin of her mother's husband. Without John the Baptist telling Israel where its rulers were going astray, they must have felt they could carry on living their decadent lives.

Wouldn't it be wonderful to be able to do that—to be able to have our every earthly desire fulfilled and never be bothered by the voice of conscience?

Perhaps. For a while. But Herod, Herodias, and her daughter would eventually have had to answer to the ultimate voice of conscience—God. And His judgment on their lives and values would last a whole lot longer than their actual lives did.

Most of us aren't raised in luxury like Herodias's daughter and, as a result, we (hopefully) have values we can face the Lord with. That's the point of hard knocks and not always getting what we want. Those times teach us what matters.

And when we learn to value the things that God gives us over and above what the world gives us, then we can dance like Herodias's daughter, but for joy and appreciation rather than personal gain. And no one need die.

THE SOLDIERS WHO CRUCIFIED CHRIST—
Power the Easy Way

Then the governor's soldiers took Jesus into the Praetorium and gathered the whole company of soldiers around him. They stripped him and put a scarlet robe on him, and then twisted together a crown of thorns and set it on his head. They put a staff in his right hand. Then they knelt in front of him and mocked him. "Hail, king of the Jews!" they said. They spit on him, and took the staff and struck him on the head again and again.

MATTHEW 27:27–30 NIV

❧

We sell ourselves very cheaply at times.

Pilate's soldiers had Jesus in their power (or so they thought). More concerned with their own position than the life of another man, they surrounded Him and mocked Him. There was no need for that. They had already flogged Him. He would have been bloodied and staggering. But perhaps they felt it enhanced their status among their peers. Perhaps they vied with each other to see who could be the cruelest.

For their own entertainment they dressed Him as a king, mocked Him, and beat Him. Were their lives so dominated and dictated by their officers that they got actual pleasure out of mocking someone who seemed even less in control

> *Dear Lord, the world has a way of making us feel worthless if we don't conform to its standard. Those standards might not seem right to us—but what else are we supposed to do? It's the world we live in. Yes, it's the world we live in—but not the one we are destined to live in forever. Stay nearby as others mock us for walking with You. Your Word is worth more than all the promises of the world.*

than they normally were?

Parading Him through the streets of Jerusalem, they would have pushed people aside. They grabbed Simon the Cyrene and forced him to carry the cross for Christ. They must have felt very powerful. Real men!

They nailed Him to the cross as they would have done with so many others and then they played games. Perhaps they were pretending to each other that they were so tough such suffering didn't even touch them.

In the end, they walked away from the cross with their reputation for toughness enhanced, their day's pay, and the clothes they took from the back of a traveling preacher. But all the while they held the treasure of heaven in their hands and didn't know it.

In a way—when we talk down the church, when we complain about what faith asks of us, when we criticize the pastor who is trying his best—we follow the soldiers' example. It is easier to join in with the voices raised in negativity than to stand against them. It is easier to be one of the gang than it is to stand alone before God. But when we do so, the devil pays us off cheaply and laughs at what we might have taken away from the cross—but didn't.

THE MAGI—
Wiser Men after the Event

After Jesus was born in Bethlehem in Judea, during the time of King Herod,
Magi from the east came to Jerusalem and asked, "Where is the one who has been
born king of the Jews? We saw his star when it rose and have come to worship
him." When King Herod heard this he was disturbed, and all Jerusalem with him.

MATTHEW 2:1–3 NIV

Despite a later tradition identifying them as Caspar (or Gaspar), Balthazar, and Melchior, the Gospel writer Matthew never actually names the wise men from the east who pay homage to the baby Jesus.

They are referred to as "magi" or "kings," but all we actually know about them is that they were wise men. We don't even know how many of them there were, although the fact that they presented three gifts suggests that there may have been three of them.

How likely is it that these wise men from the east might have predicted the birth of the king of the Jews in time to make the long journey to greet him? Quite likely, actually. Even Herod's priests seem to have known of the predictions, although we can understand why they wouldn't choose to mention them to him. What is a little more fantastical, though, is the nature of the star they followed. It seems to have moved in front of them, guiding them to a specific location. (Try that some time. Follow a star and see where it takes you.)

> Lord Jesus, how can we ever know if we are really following You or simply doing what our friends do or what we were raised to do? How do we know we have a real relationship with You? If we haven't already felt Your power change our lives, then change us now, Lord. Make our tomorrows more Christ filled than our yesterdays. Turn our "traveling" hearts heavenward.

Of course, God might have illuminated their journey in any number of ways.

The gifts they offered the Christ-child, according to the Church Father Origen, are symbolic, being "gold for a king; myrrh as to one who is mortal and incense as to a god." Of course, Jesus would have had all these attributes already; the gifts may have been an acknowledgment of the fact.

So, what do the wise men teach us? We needn't search Jesus out; we needn't travel to find Him. Gregory the Great, who lived in the sixth century, tells us we might learn from the way they departed. Having been questioned by Herod as they arrived, the wise men decide to return home by another route. Perhaps they felt they were in danger, even though these would have been powerful and influential men. But, as Gregory says, having found Jesus, their lives would never be the same. Everything changed, and they could never go back to their old ways again.

Having found Jesus, we walk a new path, and the powers of the earth can pursue us if they like. We are heading not eastward but heavenward.

THE GOOD SAMARITAN—
The Hands of the Lord

But a certain Samaritan, as he journeyed, came where he was: and when he saw
him, he had compassion on him, and went to him, and bound up his wounds,
pouring in oil and wine, and set him on his own beast, and brought him to an
inn, and took care of him. And on the morrow when he departed, he took out
two pence, and gave them to the host, and said unto him, Take care of him;
and whatsoever thou spendest more, when I come again, I will repay thee.

LUKE 10:33–35 KJV

⊱⊰

Jesus never said the name of the Good Samaritan, but even His use of that phrase would have made His audience pay attention. The Samaritans, as far as the Jews were concerned, were a debased, outcast people. They had mingled their bloodlines with that of the conquering Assyrians and worshipped Jehovah in a different way! This enmity had existed for generations.

The idea that a Samaritan might be good—and better than a priest or a Levite—would have been a shocking one.

A man had been robbed, beaten, and left by the roadside—a scenario as familiar these days as it was then. Two men, supposed upholders of the law and bastions of the faith, saw him and walked on by. A third man—someone the beaten man himself may not have stopped to help because of his nationality and way of worshipping—bathed him, bandaged him, and took him to an inn, paying for his lodgings and care. Then he

> *Lord Jesus, the fact that You never even mentioned the name of the Samaritan but he became known around the world and across the centuries for being an example of Your love should tell us something. To be Your hands in this world of troubles is a prize worth more than any amount of fame.*

went about his business.

Of the three passersby, Jesus reserves His praise for the least likely candidate—a man Jesus Himself, as a Jew, should have had nothing to do with.

So, what was the point He was making? Perhaps this—that God cares little for our nationality or our place of worship (the Samaritans refused to worship at the temple in Jerusalem). He doesn't care if we are rich (as the priest and the Levite undoubtedly were) or poor. And He certainly doesn't care what other people say about us.

What matters most to God is summed up perfectly by Jesus when He said, "Love God and one another." Everything else is man-made and superfluous.

The Samaritan's actions are offered in response to a question about achieving eternal life. The person who asked the question doesn't seem to have had a response. But we can. We can follow that example on our way to eternal life—and make this world a little more like heaven by our actions as we go, no matter who we might be or what other people think of us.

THE GIRL POSSESSED BY A DIVINING SPIRIT—
Demons Proclaim Salvation

Once when we were going to the place of prayer, we were met by a
female slave who had a spirit by which she predicted the future.
She earned a great deal of money for her owners by fortune-telling.
She followed Paul and the rest of us, shouting, "These men are servants
of the Most High God, who are telling you the way to be saved."
ACTS 16:16–17 NIV

⎯⎯◦◦◦⎯⎯

The apostle Paul and his entourage were traveling near the city of Philippi, meeting with believers and spreading the Gospel to others, when they attracted a new and troublesome companion.

She was young, a slave, and a moneymaker for her masters. People believed her to be possessed by a demon who could tell the future, and they paid well to listen to her ravings. But she gained a particular focus when Paul arrived. For several days, she followed the Christian group around, shouting, telling everyone they were servants of God who held the keys to salvation.

It sounds like praise, but it may have been sarcasm. It may have been the demon speaking or her soul proclaiming a fact it recognized and yearned for. Whatever it was, Paul confronted her, addressed the demon, and cast it out in Jesus' name.

The effectiveness of his actions were testified to by her owners. Men who made financial gain from

> *Dear Lord, You know that the ones who most need help, who most need to hear Your Word, are often the most difficult to reach. In fact, their behavior might make us want to back away rather than reach out. Give us a heart to reach out to the hard-to-reach cases. And keep us safe when we do.*

a troubled young woman would surely have little time for the words of an itinerant preacher, but they rushed Paul to court for destroying their livelihood.

It isn't stated, but the effect on the girl must have been dramatic. She would have been restored to normal life—and been of no further use to her owners. What happened to her next goes unrecorded, but it is hoped the women who traveled with Paul welcomed her into the fold.

Her name may never have been recorded, but she was surely at the forefront of the battle between good and evil, being occupied by one of those forces and liberated by the other. Perhaps by the fact that she followed Paul from place to place making a nuisance of herself we can guess that even demons want to be redeemed. Or that whatever power Satan had over her, it was not complete enough to prevent her from reaching out for help.

The next time we are confronted by someone who really annoys us, someone determined to get in our way, we might remember this girl and wonder, *Is this someone I should just avoid for the sake of peace and quiet, or is this someone I could help set free?*

THE WOMAN WHO BLED
FOR TWELVE YEARS—
Daughter of the Lord

Just then a woman who had been subject to bleeding for twelve years came up
behind him and touched the edge of his cloak. She said to herself, "If I only touch
his cloak, I will be healed." Jesus turned and saw her. "Take heart, daughter,"
he said, "your faith has healed you." And the woman was healed at that moment.
MATTHEW 9:20–22 NIV

Imagine bleeding for twelve long years! This woman must have been exhausted and emaciated. Medical science, such as it was in those days, was unable to help and may actually have made her health worse. Her illness impoverished her life physically and financially. On top of all that, there was the stigma of uncleanliness that Jewish law attached to such bleeding. After twelve years of this she must have felt there was no hope for her. Then she heard about Jesus!

Those of us with a heart to help, Father, can sometimes think that the entire burden of restoring others rests on our efforts. And, according to Your Son, Jesus, those efforts are not unimportant. But, while we do what we can, keep us always aware that You can do more. Your daughters and sons are best helped by their heavenly Father. Give us the strength to help them where we can and to direct them to You for the rest.

Going out in public, and unaccompanied as far as we know, she pushed her way through the crowd, not daring to think He might speak to her, but in the certainty that the merest touch of His cloak would be enough to cure her. It was!

This faith-filled woman goes unnamed in the Bible, but there is another unnamed (and unmentioned) person in her story. The one who told her about Jesus. The one who filled her with the certainty that He could and would help her.

"If I just touch His clothes I will be healed," she said. Who told her that?

The journey to faith is a difficult one for many. Those who already know the Lord can make that journey more difficult or more attractive for others by the way we live and the words we speak. This other unnamed person spoke the words that convinced a sick and supposedly unclean woman not only to leave her house but to struggle to reach the Lord. Whoever he or she was, they convinced the woman that her efforts would be rewarded, that she would be healed.

When Jesus turned to the woman, she explained what happened. As Jesus replied that she was already healed, He shows us how unimportant our worldly names really are. He called her "daughter."

We can be like the unknown encourager, and we can be like the unnamed woman and reach out in our need and our faith. But however we behave and whatever name we possess, we could not do better than have Jesus, at the end, call us "daughter" or "son."

THE WOMAN WHO
BLESSED JESUS' MOTHER—
Gently Redirected

And it came to pass, as he spake these things, a certain woman of the company
lifted up her voice, and said unto him, Blessed is the womb that bare thee,
and the paps which thou hast sucked. But he said, Yea rather,
blessed are they that hear the word of God, and keep it.

LUKE 11:27–28 KJV

❈

Jesus had been busy! He had been teaching the Lord's Prayer, driving out demons, and preaching powerfully to many people. People gathered from miles around. Listeners and watchers were caught up in all the excitement. At one point a woman in the crowd, overcome with enthusiasm, cried out a blessing on the mother who gave this wonderful prophet to the world.

In previous eras that might have been a perfectly acceptable thing to say, other prophets might have appreciated it, but Jesus, with no disrespect to Mary, immediately redirected her praise to the Word of God and blessed those who obey it.

A useful reminder to her, and to us.

How many people cheer at a parade but have never been involved in setting one up? How many have waited with

> *Dear Lord, when we seem to achieve things for Your kingdom, when we help the hungry or the poor. . .it feels good. We might be tempted to feel pleased with ourselves. If we are involved in church programs, those who run them can seem like people we should aspire to emulate. If we are helped by programs or individuals, we might be tempted to direct our thanks towards them. But You, Lord, are the power, the inspiration, and the provider. All praise goes to You.*

eager anticipation for the beginning of hockey season but have never pulled on a pair of skates? How many talk to their friends about last night's installment of their favorite TV program but would have no idea how such a thing comes together?

It's one thing to stand and cheer, to get excited about what others are doing, to support someone who's doing what you aren't/can't/won't. The kingdom of heaven isn't like that. You are either in or you are out. Standing on the sidelines throwing out blessings doesn't count, or if it does, it counts as "out."

Jesus' mother was certainly worthy of praise. Perhaps the woman who shouted was a mother as well and simply wanted to show her appreciation of a job very well done. But Mary was a woman true to her faith. Her greatest glory came from being a humble servant of God. She needed no more blessings than those already provided by God.

Jesus reminded the enthusiastic woman in the crowd that we all need to be like His mother, obedient to the Word of God. Once we begin that walk for real, there will be no more standing by cheering someone on. We will be in the game. . .active participants in the kingdom of heaven. And no other blessings are required.

THE MAN WITH LEPROSY—
Coming Out of Hiding

When Jesus came down from the mountainside, large crowds followed him.
A man with leprosy came and knelt before him and said, "Lord, if you are
willing, you can make me clean." Jesus reached out his hand and touched the man.
"I am willing," he said. "Be clean!" Immediately he was cleansed of his leprosy.
MATTHEW 8:1–3 NIV

⸺⸺

Jesus had just finished teaching what would be passed down to us as the Sermon on the Mount, a collection of His most definitive teachings. The people who heard Him were stunned and confused by this man's wisdom and authority. No doubt they milled around discussing the things He had said for some time after it was all finished.

Into that throng walked a brave man, giving us one of the simplest statements of faith in the whole Bible.

Father God, a facial deformity might hide a loyal, faithful heart, and a beautiful complexion might shelter a twisted soul. Teach us to have less concern for the superficial and to focus more on the essence of the person. May we seek always to find You in others and recognize that You might be at work in the most unexpected of places and behind the least likely faces. And should we be in hiding or be wounded by the world, may we have the courage to reach out to You.

The man was a leper. As such he would not have been allowed to mingle with "normal" people. Lepers were often confined to separate communities and fed from a distance by those who loved them and were brave enough to maintain contact in the face of massive social stigma.

This man may have heard Jesus speaking before, or news of the many healings may have reached him. Something gave him the faith to be there that day. He may have been covered up, but he risked a lot by doing what he did.

He approached Jesus directly, exposed his leprosy, and his heart, by stating simply that Jesus could heal him. Jesus' reply is as simple and as heartfelt as the request.

In touching him to heal him no doubt Jesus understood his anguish and the years of isolation prescribed by the law. So, He sent him to the temple to tell the priests and make the required offering of thanks. No doubt this was a rebuke to the priests who had failed this man and shut him out.

Leprosy is still a problem in the world, but it is generally considered that the term used in the Bible covered a multitude of skin diseases. Whether he was terribly deformed or suffered from superficial blemishes, Jesus' response to his faith-filled request would have been the same.

Those of us who are spared obvious physical deformities will still have deformities of the heart. Like leprosy, those problems will show themselves in many different ways. But if we take them to the Lord in simple faith, convinced that He can heal us, then He will!

THE RICH YOUNG MAN—
Preferred the Good Life
instead of the God Life

"All these I have kept," the young man said. "What do I still lack?" Jesus
answered, "If you want to be perfect, go, sell your possessions and give to the
poor, and you will have treasure in heaven. Then come, follow me." When the
young man heard this, he went away sad, because he had great wealth.
MATTHEW 19:20–22 NIV

⬥

People generally loved, hated, or were confused by Jesus. Very few approached Him sincerely and walked away from Him afterward. The rich young man—or the rich young ruler—was one of those people. Such an event might seem pointless—hardly worth giving space to in the Bible—but Jesus used it to make a powerful point.

The young man seemed to have written himself a checklist for attaining eternal life. But he wanted to double-check, and so he asked Jesus what good things he must do. Jesus told him that he needs to keep the commandments: not murder, not steal, honor his parents, not commit adultery, not lie, and love his neighbor as himself.

"I've kept them all!" he said, surely expecting an instant ticket to immortality. Even the disciples seemed impressed by him. But Jesus, who knows a man's soul better than the man does himself, rounded off the list by going straight for the man's sin.

Dear Lord, we must not see our encounter with You as something to check on our "bucket list." Meeting You is the only thing. It will completely alter our priorities, showing us the true value of material things. If we value anything more than You, give us the courage to clear it away or to let You sweep it from our lives. Lord, let it be You and only You that we worship.

"Sell all you have," He said. "Then follow Me."

Now, suddenly, the man probably felt hard done by. That kind of command might be okay for poor folk who don't have much to sell, but he had a lot of possessions. Surely that's not a fair request to make of someone like him! And so he went off to reconsider this eternal life thing.

Jesus probably couldn't have cared less about the man's property, but He knew wealth and possessions were the young man's true love and He would not—could not—take second place to that.

We are allowed to own property. We are allowed to make a lot of money. But with Jesus at the head of our list of priorities we won't be able to help putting that property and money to good use. If we don't, if we keep it for ourselves and our own use, then it becomes our very own false idol, the thing that comes between us and God or eternal life.

Such things might provide us with a comfortable life in this world, but try asking them to love you, forgive you, and keep you with them forever and ever. Like the rich young man, you will be in for a bitter disappointment.

THE BLIND AND
MUTE DEMONIAC—
Lost as a Man Could Be

But they, when they were departed, spread abroad his fame in all that country.
As they went out, behold, they brought to him a dumb man possessed with a
devil. And when the devil was cast out, the dumb spake: and the multitudes
marvelled, saying, It was never so seen in Israel. But the Pharisees said,
He casteth out devils through the prince of the devils.

MATTHEW 9:31–34 KJV

If ever there was a lost soul, it was the man referred to as the Demoniac. He was blind, he couldn't speak, and he was said to be possessed by a demon. What remained of the real man must have felt that his life was an actual living, walking hell.

Jesus had come from a confrontation where He showed the Pharisees that He was indeed willing to heal on the Sabbath. Now He was the only hope for a man all but cut off from the good of the world. Still, someone must have cared enough for him to bring him to Jesus.

This man could neither see the Lord nor ask Him for help. Because of the state of his mind, whether through conventional insanity (as some might think) or actual demonic possession, he was in no position to ask for help or

> *Almighty God, we make excuses. We will do better when. . . We will do it differently after. . . We can't come to God because. . . We will go to church when we get. . . It's a very human and very frustrating failing, and it's what we need to overcome. The problem isn't Yours. You will come into the ugly, embarrassing, painful depths of our pain and captivity to set us free. All we need to do is stop making excuses.*

even to want it. But the Lord restored him.

We aren't told if any words were spoken (presumably, the Demoniac could still hear) or what actions were taken. The healing is mentioned almost in passing, like a casual thing requiring no noticeable effort.

The Pharisees were once again outraged, insisting Jesus was in league with the devil. Tired of their carping, Jesus told them that the devil would not work against his own forces and if He was actually doing God's work, then they should know that their time was up. The kingdom of God truly was at hand.

In the battle between good and evil, the Pharisees had picked the wrong side. In reclaiming a man believed taken by the devil—something the Pharisees could never have done—He had not only shown them on which side the power lay, but He also gave a man his life back.

If the ex-Demoniac could speak to us today, he would surely have one, all-important message for us—no matter how lost we might be, how close to hell we might have been dragged, or how much Satan might think he owns us, Jesus can bring us back.

THE BOY WHO
GAVE HIS LUNCH—
But Didn't Go Hungry

One of his disciples, Andrew, Simon Peter's brother, saith unto him,
There is a lad here, which hath five barley loaves, and two small fishes:
but what are they among so many? And Jesus said, Make the men sit down.
Now there was much grass in the place. So the men sat down, in number
about five thousand. And Jesus took the loaves; and when he had given thanks,
he distributed to the disciples, and the disciples to them that were set down;
and likewise of the fishes as much as they would.

JOHN 6:8–11 KJV

He is a pivotal character in one of the greatest stories ever told, but no one knows his name. In three of the four Gospels that tell the story, he isn't even mentioned.

Only John tells us that Jesus fed five thousand people with one little boy's lunch.

> It's a simple thing, Lord, but it goes against all common sense. You put us in positions where what is required is more than we could possibly provide. That's when many of us turn away. Stay our feet, give us the courage to move forward, and remind us that it is never us but You who does the providing.

In this telling, the disciple Andrew reports that the boy has five small loaves and two small fish. He wonders how so little will make a difference to all the people who had gathered to hear Jesus speak.

In three of the four Gospels, the disciples remind Jesus that the people must be fed. He tells them to see to it. Their response can be paraphrased as an astonished "How?" Even when they find a boy willing to give up his lunch, they can't imagine how that would help.

The disciples are just back from their first foray into the world without Him. They have been telling Him about the miracles they had done and the things they taught. Perhaps His challenge to them in suggesting they feed the multitude was His way of seeing how far they had come—or showing them how far they had to go.

The boy seems to have offered up his bread and fish without objection and without worry. Of course Jesus manages to feed five thousand people with it and still have plenty left over.

In life, we will face challenges that seem impossible. Like the disciples, we might throw up our hands in despair and insist it can't be done. But the proper response should be like the response of the unnamed boy. He offered up what he had, gave it over to Jesus, and trusted Him to make of it what needed to be made.

So, before deciding any good thing might be impossible to achieve, make a start in whatever way you can with whatever you have and trust that Jesus will see you through to completion. You might well be amazed by what He makes of your "impossible" task.

THE GALILEANS WHOSE
BLOOD PILATE MIXED
WITH THEIR SACRIFICES—
Knew Not the Hour

Now there were some present at that time who told Jesus about the Galileans
whose blood Pilate had mixed with their sacrifices. Jesus answered, "Do you think
that these Galileans were worse sinners than all the other Galileans because they
suffered this way? I tell you, no! But unless you repent, you too will all perish."
LUKE 13:1–3 NIV

All we know about these unfortunate Galileans is what the people in the crowd mentioned to Jesus—that the Roman governor mixed their blood with their sacrifices. The incident isn't referred to anywhere else in scripture, but we can justifiably make certain assumptions and, as always, learn from Jesus' response.

History tells us that Pontius Pilate was not the most tolerant of rulers. He was likely to send his soldiers into the streets at the slightest provocation. Seen as indecisive at the trial of Jesus, he was often quick to resort to deadly force with the general population. (But, of course, Jesus was a special case.)

On occasion Pilate also openly looted the temple's coffers of money given as an offering to God for his various building projects.

> It comes down to this. Life is fleeting and serves only one purpose. While we are passing through this world, we ought to be living examples of God's love and bring as many as we can to Him. But the only thing that counts in the end is whether we truly knew and accepted Jesus as our Savior. Lord, help us prepare for the unexpected by placing all our trust in the one certainty this life offers us—You!

Some would willingly turn a blind eye to this, but others would be outraged—and would generally pay for that outrage with their lives!

It seems that on this occasion some Jews who had traveled from Galilee to make their blood sacrifice (perhaps doves or a lamb) were slain in front of the altar so their blood flowed over their offering.

What their offence was we do not know, but it was obviously a matter of speculation for those telling the story, wondering what their sin had been for such a brutal end to come upon them.

Jesus, refusing as always to get involved in earthly politics, more or less points out that these things happen. It didn't mean these men were worse sinners than anyone else. It was just life—and death—in Israel at that time.

He seems to suggest that how and when we die isn't all that important. What is important is that we have turned to God before it happens so we might have eternal life afterward.

Those Galileans probably had no idea that the hour of their death was at hand. Very few of us do. So, doesn't it make sense to prepare beforehand? Let's make our lives a living offering to God so that when and if our blood is spilled, we will already be His.

THE MAN WHO LIVED
IN THE TOMBS—
From Living Death to Eternal Life

And always, night and day, he was in the mountains, and in the tombs, crying, and cutting himself with stones. But when he saw Jesus afar off, he ran and worshipped him, and cried with a loud voice, and said, What have I to do with thee, Jesus, thou Son of the most high God? I adjure thee by God, that thou torment me not. For he said unto him, Come out of the man, thou unclean spirit.
MARK 5:5–8 KJV

The idea of a demon-possessed man living among the tombs seems like something out of a Gothic horror movie—but it is every bit as relevant today as it was in biblical times.

People ruled by their own personal demons (i.e., drink and drugs) will live in some pretty run-down places, the kinds of places most of us would be reluctant to visit. Their behavior might well be scary and dangerous, and society's response will often be quite similar to the biblical example of binding and chaining.

Despite being possessed by a legion of demons, this man still had enough of himself in there to rail against his situation, to shout day and night, and to harm himself in frustration. There was a real battle happening inside him.

When he saw Jesus, he actually ran quite a distance toward Him and fell to his

> Almighty God, often in our fear and lack of faith we treat others in ways You would not wish. But we tell ourselves they asked for it because of their behavior. Really, we ask, what else were we supposed to do? What we are supposed to do is take chances, put ourselves in that place of vulnerability and uncertainty where Your works seem to have greatest scope.
> God, give us the courage to reach out to the difficult ones.

knees—although then the demons do the talking.

Once cured—or set free—this man's gratitude eclipsed most of those whom Jesus healed. He wanted to become a disciple. Through his struggles, possession, and "rebirth," he probably understood God and the devil better than any of the disciples. So, Jesus sent him out as a missionary.

If this man had been completely in the control of the devil, he would have been a smoother operator, calmer, more insidious. But he was fighting for his life, and that's what scared the townspeople. That fight continues to this day. The people living "in the tombs" are often scary. But that's only because there is something inside them still reacting against their situation, still blaming the world for a pain they know they shouldn't be suffering.

The people who lived nearby in their fear merely added to the pain. Jesus, in His love, wiped it all away. He didn't keep His distance. He went in among the tombs, down among the dead if you like. Where better to present someone with new life in this world and the promise of eternal life in the next?

THE MAN WHO WAS "NOT ONE OF US"—
But Was Still Doing God's Work

And John answered him, saying, Master, we saw one casting out devils in thy name, and he followeth not us: and we forbad him, because he followeth not us. But Jesus said, Forbid him not: for there is no man which shall do a miracle in my name, that can lightly speak evil of me. For he that is not against us is on our part.
MARK 9:38–40 KJV

❦

The disciples were a very special group of men selected by Jesus. But sometimes they did think a little too much of themselves—like when they argued over who would be the leader among them, or when they prevented a man from casting out demons because he wasn't a disciple.

By this time Jesus' fame had spread. He had performed many wonders and taught thousands of people. It would be surprising indeed if more than a few hadn't walked away deeply impacted and decided to try this kingdom of heaven for themselves. They may not have wanted to be a disciple. They may never have been invited. But Jesus wasn't preaching an exclusive club. His message was inclusive.

Jesus put His followers right with a few words. This man was doing miracles in His name. How could that be wrong?

The disciples' instinctive

> It's not about the church. It's not about the rituals. Lord, we need to use these earthly things for the good that is in them but never let them take the place in our hearts that rightly belongs to You. And when we meet "the stranger," help us see beyond the labels they carry to the worship in their hearts and the works of their hands. The Church is each of us joined together through You—regardless of the church we attend.

action is reflected in the number of Christian denominations we have in the world today. Each, perhaps, focusing on a different aspect of the Gospel. Each, perhaps, worshipping with different traditions, some emphasizing good works, some relying more heavily on prayer. But all of them loving the Lord.

Too often we look at these different groups and focus on the things they do that we don't do, or the priorities they have that we don't agree with. Then, because of those differences, we decide they are "not one of us." Sometimes people go even further and decide that if they are not "for us," they must be "against us." The result of these judgments? The Body of Christ suffers.

We can assume from this passage that Jesus doesn't care what church we attend. He's not overly concerned with which group we belong to. (There will never have been a group closer to Jesus than the disciples.) He cares about what we do in His name, not what others think about what we do. And if we truly act in His name according to His Word, then our works will be worthy of His approval. No matter how we worship on a Sunday.

THE SHEPHERDS—
The First to Visit the Lord

And there were shepherds living out in the fields nearby, keeping watch over their flocks at night. An angel of the Lord appeared to them, and the glory of the Lord shone around them, and they were terrified. But the angel said to them, "Do not be afraid. I bring you good news that will cause great joy for all the people."
LUKE 2:8–10 NIV

When a princess of the British royal family—and surely every other royal family—gives birth, the first person to be told (other than the father and those present) is the monarch. Then, the members of the press are gathered for the proud prince to announce his child to the world's media, who then bounce their words and images off satellites to almost every country in the world.

Imagine if instead the prince sent for the hospital cleaning staff, or the people who worked in the sandwich shop down the road, or the local street sweepers and invited them to be the first to visit his newborn child.

As huge of an upset of normal conventions as that might be, it doesn't begin to compare with the difference between what we might have expected from the birth of the Son of God and the reality. God the Father could have gathered the crowned heads of the world together to witness the arrival of His Son. Every priest in every nation could have been made aware of such a momentous event. This would have been nothing

> Shepherds, plumbers, beauticians, CEOs, philanthropists, street sweepers, even politicians—Lord, Your gift was for everyone. Presenting Your Son first to humble farm workers reminds us it isn't the job that is important, or the money in the bank, or the influence we wield, but the humility in our hearts.

less than what the world would expect from the birth of God's Son.

Instead He sent His messengers to a group of shepherds on a nearby hillside. God could not have expected them to take the news to the great powers. But He could expect them to tell the common folk, their own people. This, from the very beginning of His time on earth, told us what Jesus would be about. He would be no respecter of titles, money, or influence. He would be there to help, to heal, to teach. . .whoever was willing to be helped, be healed, and be taught. His life would be spent with the people who hadn't been separated from God by love of their possessions.

The shepherds are never mentioned again in the Bible. We have no idea how they spent the next thirty years until Jesus took up His ministry. Perhaps they played a further role in His life, or perhaps they were simply happier shepherds, having been privileged to see God begin His plan of redemption.

One thing is sure. As with everyone who meets Jesus and accepts Him as the Son of God, their lives would never be the same again.

THE MAN WHO OWNED
THE COLT—
Prepared in Advance?

As they approached Jerusalem and came to Bethphage and Bethany at the Mount of Olives, Jesus sent two of his disciples, saying to them, "Go to the village ahead of you, and just as you enter it, you will find a colt tied there, which no one has ever ridden. Untie it and bring it here. If anyone asks you, 'Why are you doing this?' say, 'The Lord needs it and will send it back here shortly.'"

MARK 11:1–3 NIV

Jesus and the Bible are a little vague about the owners of the colt. Prophecy stated that the Messiah would enter the Holy City on a donkey's colt, and Jesus was preparing to do exactly that. He seems to have known ahead of time where the particular colt He would ride was located.

Had He made arrangements in advance? It's doubtful. He traveled with an entourage of close friends and they seemed to be completely in the dark about the colt when He mentions it. They were unaware of any supporters in the area. He didn't tell the disciples whom they should ask for the use of the animal. He simply said that if anyone asks, they should say the Lord needed the animal.

Was He simply relying on the force of His name and reputation, or, as the Son of God, did He simply know

> Dear Lord, when You have it in mind to help someone, You may involve several people in the process, but Your priority is the good of the person You set out to help—not explaining the process to everyone involved along the way. It is a rare treat to see the end result of the things You ask of us, but we need to be prepared to play our part, trusting that it will work out Your way in the end. Let playing our part always be enough for us.

what was going to happen ahead of time?

Of course, someone did ask. The disciples invoked the name of the Lord—and, astonishingly, the colt was freely given. So, who was this man (or woman) who so freely gave away livestock?

A sensible person might have worried about the safety of his property. Livestock cost money and indicated status. A man's animals were rarely unimportant to him. But this little animal was handed over to someone who was viwed by many as a rabble-rouser. It was a risky move, and there was no guarantee the animal would be returned.

The owner of this beast was not sensible—whoever he was, he was more than that! Either he was forewarned by God and he listened when God spoke, or his faith was such that he recognized God's work even when presented to him by strangers. What would it be like to live such a life that we would hand our property over to strangers simply because they said Jesus needed it?

That's not sensible. That's trust. That's faith.

THE TRAVELER HELPED BY THE GOOD SAMARITAN—
Inducted into Mystery

In reply Jesus said: "A man was going down from Jerusalem to Jericho, when he
was attacked by robbers. They stripped him of his clothes, beat him and went away,
leaving him half dead. A priest happened to be going down the same road,
and when he saw the man, he passed by on the other side. So too, a Levite,
when he came to the place and saw him, passed by on the other side. But a Samaritan,
as he traveled, came where the man was; and when he saw him, he took pity on him."
LUKE 10:30–33 NIV

We know next to nothing about the man who was robbed in the story of the Good Samaritan. He was traveling from Jerusalem to Jericho. He may have been a worshipper at the temple (and as such would have been poorer after leaving Jerusalem), or he may have been a trader (and as such, a rich target).

We do know that the road from Jerusalem to Jericho went through dangerous terrain with steep hills and ravines running alongside the track. Perfect ambush territory! The man probably never knew what hit him. Then, after the robbers had left and he was as low as he could possibly be, he entered the mystery of God's love.

The Samaritan, who we know was carrying wine and oil and would have been at risk of being robbed himself, stepped into the traveler's

Awesome God, You are an
undeserved gift, a gift mankind
could never hope to deserve.
Perhaps because we are
surrounded by it, we take it for
granted. Forgive us, Lord, and
increase the appreciation in our
hearts. You are worthy of our every
breath being spent in praise. Help
us to realize it in the many good
times as well as the bad.

world of trouble and became the source of his healing, his help, his very life. He must have thought he deserved none of this—and yet he was receiving it all for free.

The Samaritan tended to him, traveled with him, and even when their ways parted, the Samaritan left provision for him.

Wow! How must this man have responded to such unexpected generosity? Perhaps, when he was restored to health, he went in search of his benefactor. We can be sure he told everyone who would listen about his savior.

The traveler must have been very confused. And amazed. That is what it is like to be present in the mystery of God's love.

We are all in that place, but we often only realize it when we are beaten down—when we are metaphorically lying by the roadside. It might be smart to try and appreciate that before we hit rock bottom. Then, aware of the mystery and the immensity of it all, we might search for the source of that love and do what the man on the road to Jericho must surely have done—tell everyone we meet about it!

ICHABOD'S MOTHER—
Losing All Hope

And about the time of her death the women that stood by her said unto her,
Fear not; for thou hast born a son. But she answered not, neither did she regard it.
And she named the child Ichabod, saying, The glory is departed from Israel: because
the ark of God was taken, and because of her father in law and her husband.

1 SAMUEL 4:20–21 KJV

The name Ichabod means "the glory is departed from Israel." How desperate would you have to be to give your child such a name? And how inconsiderate?

Ichabod's mother's appearance in the Bible is brief and tragic. Near her time of delivery, she heard the ark of the covenant had been captured by the Philistines, and her husband and father-in-law had died. She went into early labor, saddled her newborn son with a hopeless name, and then died. Of despair, apparently.

Tragic circumstances, no doubt. But let's look at them another way. The ark of the covenant (and the power within it) was more than capable of taking care of itself. It once killed a man who touched it when he shouldn't have. The real loss in its capture was Israel's national pride.

The loss of her husband and father-in-law might have been a more serious blow. This woman doesn't seem to have had anyone else to turn to. Perhaps her

Dear Lord, one of the most difficult things to do is to find hope in seemingly hopeless situations. We need to understand that the people and the things that make up our earthly lives are Yours to give, take away, or rearrange. Endow us with enough understanding to watch You work, trusting that You have it all under control. Teach us to not fear and to understand that Your glory goes on forever and ever. Amen.

husband's unpopularity had something to do with that. Phinehas, the son of Eli, was known to steal from the tabernacle offerings and have his way with the female servants. She may only have stayed with him because of the lifestyle he and his father, the high priest, provided. It might have been the loss of that lifestyle more than anything that caused her despair.

Position and possessions can do that to us. When they are taken from us, it can be all too easy to think the world (as we know it) has come to an end. And so she gave her son that desolate name.

The glory that had left Israel was certainly not God's glory, despite the loss of the ark. God's glory is everywhere, from rising sun to rising sun, all around the world. Its constant gift is the promise of a new day, a new beginning, better times.

If Ichabod's mother had been more concerned with God, she would have understood her earthly situation was purely temporary—no matter how severe her loss, there would always be hope in Him.

God's glory in our lives is not so easily lost.

JOSEPH'S GUIDE INTO SLAVERY—
At the Right Place,
at the Right Time

*So he said to him, "Go and see if all is well with your brothers and with the
flocks, and bring word back to me." Then he sent him off from the Valley of
Hebron. When Joseph arrived at Shechem, a man found him wandering around
in the fields and asked him, "What are you looking for?" He replied, "I'm looking
for my brothers. Can you tell me where they are grazing their flocks?"*

GENESIS 37:14–16 NIV

Joseph had just become the proud owner of a coat of many colors,
and he decided to indulge in a little showing off. As if that wasn't
annoying enough, he then prophesied that his brothers would kneel
down before him.

Understandably, the brothers were a little annoyed, so their father
sent them off to check on the family flocks, a subtle way of allowing
time for hot heads to cool down. But, of course, the situation couldn't
be left like that, so after a suitable amount of time passed he sent
Joseph after them to make peace.

From a storytelling point of view, the next scene should be Joseph finding
his brothers. But instead, we find him standing where the brothers were supposed
to be, bewildered by their absence, until "a certain man" tells him where they are.

Of course, things go terribly wrong for Joseph

> *Father God, if our trust in Your
> grand plan is to be anywhere near
> complete, we need to understand
> that no one and nothing comes
> into our lives for no reason. If
> someone appears in our way, give
> us the faith to ask how they might
> help us—or how we might help
> them. That way we will surely
> always be traveling in the right
> direction—Your direction!*

after this—before going spectacularly right! But let's set aside the story of Joseph. Given that nothing is casually included in the Bible, perhaps we ought to think a little about this certain man.

Why was he even mentioned? Without him, Joseph might have wandered around awhile before going home. His brothers might have been too tired after a day of work to be bothered with him. Joseph might have had time to think on the error of his ways. But the certain man makes sure he finds his brothers, makes sure he is sold into slavery by them, and makes sure he will eventually save not only Egypt but his own people, as well.

The certain man might have been a messenger from God, or he might have been a stranger, completely unaware of the role he was playing. Certain men or women may have guided our lives in the past. We might have fulfilled the same role for others. The point is, in a world where God's plan is unfolding in all its detailed intricacies, people who "just happen" to be there will actually be there for a very good reason. And that reason will be God's. You can be certain of that!

THE HOST OF THE
LAST SUPPER—
An Invisible Servant

*On the first day of the Festival of Unleavened Bread, the disciples came to
Jesus and asked, "Where do you want us to make preparations for you to eat
the Passover?" He replied, "Go into the city to a certain man and tell him,
'The Teacher says: My appointed time is near. I am going to celebrate the
Passover with my disciples at your house.'" So the disciples did as
Jesus had directed them and prepared the Passover.*
MATTHEW 26:17–19 NIV

Being a servant is actually a great skill. Ask any of the butlers and
waiting staff of grand mansions and old titled families. Their purpose
is to almost efface themselves from the scene while still being visible
enough to provide the hosts whatever might be necessary whenever it
might become necessary.

The owner of the upper room where Jesus and the disciples shared
what become known as the Last Supper managed to provide what
Jesus needed on that fateful night without ever being mentioned by
name or appearing in the story. As a servant of the Son of Man who urged us to be servants, he appears to have done an excellent job!

That he knew Jesus is evident from when Jesus tells His disciples to tell the man what "the Teacher" required of him. But the disciples appear not to have known him. In the book of

> Lord, remind us as we need it
> that our fame and name stays
> behind in this world when we
> come into your kingdom. Any
> acknowledgment we receive here
> will be as nothing compared to
> Your acknowledgment of the lives
> we lived, the love we gave, and
> the service we rendered. May we
> spend our time in this world in
> Your service, not ours.

Luke, they are led to this certain man by a water carrier.

He gives over a room that is furnished and able to accommodate thirteen men (but is strangely empty at such a busy time of year) and provides food, drink, and service throughout one of the most important episodes of Jesus' ministry, and yet he is not even mentioned or referred to once the group arrives for the meal.

Human pride often demands at least an acknowledgement. But God hadn't even made this man known to Jesus' closest followers. Neither does he appear to have wanted thanks or recognition. For some, it is simply enough to serve.

In this world, such an attitude often seems weak, feeble even. But try it. It is far more difficult than might be expected. But that was the way with most of Jesus' teachings; they seemed soft—but took strong men and women to live them.

The student of the Teacher had been well taught and served Him at a pivotal time. No doubt he is very well known in heaven. The best of servants, in recognition of the difficulties of the job, are often highly sought after. Those of us who are servants of God need no recognition in this world because we also are highly sought after.

THE WIDOW AT THE TREASURY—
All She Had to Live on Was Her Faith

As Jesus looked up, he saw the rich putting their gifts into the temple treasury.
He also saw a poor widow put in two very small copper coins. "Truly I tell you," he
said, "this poor widow has put in more than all the others. All these people gave their
gifts out of their wealth; but she out of her poverty put in all she had to live on."
LUKE 21:1–4 NIV

Generally, widows seem well thought of in the Bible. Perhaps their grief brings them closer to God. Perhaps the loss in their lives leaves more space for the Lord to fill.

We are told to "take up the cause of the fatherless [and] plead the case of the widow" and instructed not to "take advantage of the widow or the fatherless" (Isaiah 1:17, Exodus 22:22 NIV). Looking after widows and orphans is considered "religion that God our Father accepts as pure and faultless" (James 1:27).

It may simply have been that—in a society where a woman's security depended on her sons or her husband—the widow was often among the poor and needy. Even so—perhaps especially so—they were not beneath the attention of their Creator.

> *Father God, remind us, as we need reminding, that we own nothing—that all we have is a gift from You. You provide what we need even when it seems to the world that we have nothing. Let us not be overly attached to or concerned with the money You send our way. And if we can offer it back to You as a token of love and thanks, may we always be willing to do that in trust and love.*

When Jesus pointed out the widow making her offering at the temple, His disciples did not know her—but He seemed to. How else would He have known that two copper coins were all she had?

How else would He have known the spirit in which she had given her offering? Perhaps because in some form—Father, Son, or Holy Spirit—He had already been with her in her grief, her loss, and her everyday struggle. Were those coins her way of thanking the Lord for His continued presence and support? Can we doubt that His love and provision for her continued after that day? Should we doubt it in our own lives?

Her offering to God was one of thanks and appreciation, even though she seemed to have little to give thanks for. Offering all she had was an outward symbol of her offering all she was. Foolishness in the eyes of the world, surely, but beautiful enough in the sight of Jesus for Him to single her out and for her example to be preserved throughout the centuries.

Many of our tithes and gifts will have far greater monetary value than this woman's two small copper coins, but how many would give the same proportion of our wealth? How many would give the same proportion of our lives?

THE MOTHER OF MICAH—
Acting in Faith but Not Really

Now a man named Micah from the hill country of Ephraim said to his mother,
"The eleven hundred shekels of silver that were taken from you and about which
I heard you utter a curse—I have that silver with me; I took it." Then his mother
said, "The LORD bless you, my son!" When he returned the eleven hundred shekels
of silver to his mother, she said, "I solemnly consecrate my silver to the LORD for
my son to make an image overlaid with silver. I will give it back to you."

JUDGES 17:1–3 NIV

———❧———

Micah's mother was acting in faith—apparently—but she doesn't seem to have paid attention to some of God's basic traits and commandments.

Firstly, she raised a son who stole from her. Okay, he owned up to it, but it may only have been the fear of a curse that made him do so. His mother was also a woman who cursed.

She praised the Lord for Micah's honesty. Then she promised her son he could have the money back—but in the form of a graven idol to worship.

Micah seems to have been so far removed from the church of the day that he actually made himself some priestly robes, hired a Levite to live with him, and set the statue up among other household gods. In essence, he started his own church, worshipping "the Lord" in the form of a statue decorated with stolen silver.

> *Almighty God, there is a reason you gave us the Bible (and the Ten Commandments before that). We are a flighty people, and we need a solid anchor in this ever-changing, ever-distracting world. Your written Word provides that for us. May we cling to it, study it, learn from it. And may we always seek to be a part of Your Church, resisting the foolish temptation to set up our own.*

The silver statue soon attracted armed men who stole it away, threatening the lives of Micah and his family as they did so. It goes on to have a long "career" as the god of the Danite people, who really should have known better.

The Bible says that "in those days...everyone did as they saw fit" (Judges 21:25 NIV). Micah's mother seems to have raised him in that sorry tradition without any firm foundations. How much better off might he—and generations of Danites—have been if his mother had understood her faith and stuck to it? Or if she had raised her son to do what was right in the eyes of God?

A little study, a little thought, a little practice and discipline—they can seem like an unnecessary nuisance at the time. It might seem easier to shape an idol than to properly shape a child's life. But there is no shortcut when it comes to living a life of faith. We need to live it—and teach it—the way God sees fit.

THE CENTURION—
A Man under Authority

The centurion replied, "Lord, I do not deserve to have you come under my roof.
But just say the word, and my servant will be healed. For I myself am a
man under authority, with soldiers under me. I tell this one, 'Go,' and he goes;
and that one, 'Come,' and he comes. I say to my servant, 'Do this,' and he does it."
MATTHEW 8:8–9 NIV

❧

Why wasn't the centurion named? He was obviously well known, and even respected. Luke tells us Jewish elders spoke up for him and that he had built a synagogue for the local population. Jesus Himself proclaimed the soldier's faith as an example to Israel. Perhaps, as a Gentile invader, his name was not thought worthy of record, but Jesus was prepared to visit this man's home.

It can hardly be that the centurion's name was unknown or that it was kept secret to preserve his safety. He himself wasn't shy or surreptitious in what he was doing.

Perhaps it wasn't mentioned because *who* he was was less important than *what* he was—a man under authority.

The centurion had soldiers under his command, soldiers whose very life or death might depend on his orders. Likewise, he was under the command of an emperor who only had to say the word and his order would become law in the greatest empire the world had ever known. He knew about the use of power. And it seems he also knew about Jesus.

> *Dear Lord above, who else should we turn to? As the Creator of heaven and earth, all power must obviously come from You. But all too often we are distracted or deceived into paying homage to local powers. Clear our minds so that we may see that the paths of power, healing, and salvation lead only to You!*

Whatever he had seen or heard of Jesus was enough for the centurion to know that He served a power strong enough to heal his servant from a distance, simply by saying that it would be so.

The healing itself may not have been such a big deal as miracles went, but the faith that requested it with the certainty that it could be done astounded the Lord.

Really, compared with his faith and understanding of who Jesus was and what He could do, the man's name was irrelevant. It may even have been a distraction. The purpose of the story being included in the Bible was not so we could be like Julius or Marcellus or Aquilinus or whatever the centurion's name was. The idea is that we, too, should seek to become people under God's authority first and foremost, no matter how little or how much authority we might have of our own.

Neither the centurion nor his emperor could have healed the servant he was so fond of, so he went to where real power walked the earth and he asked in humility. And it was done.

THE PARALYZED MAN—
Healed Twice

"Which is easier: to say, 'Your sins are forgiven,' or to say, 'Get up and walk'?
But I want you to know that the Son of Man has authority on earth to forgive
sins." So he said to the paralyzed man, "Get up, take your mat and go home."
Then the man got up and went home. When the crowd saw this, they were filled
with awe; and they praised God, who had given such authority to man.
MATTHEW 9:5–8 NIV

❦

Jesus had been busy healing the sick, calming storms, driving out demons, but with one anonymous man, almost in passing He raised the stakes dramatically.

Some men (we don't know who they were or even how many of them there were) brought a paralyzed friend to Jesus. Seeing them, and understanding what they had done, He is impressed by their faith. So, what does He do? Does He heal the man? No. He forgives him of his sins.

Now that may seem like simple, possibly empty, words. But to the listening Pharisees it was blasphemy, and to Jesus' followers it was a statement of identity. Both sides knew that only God could forgive sins. Those few words would have been earth-shaking at that time and place.

> *Dear Lord, we ask for all sorts of things in our prayers. We ask to make deadlines, we ask that this infection might clear, we ask for happiness, we ask for success, we ask help for others, we ask for healing. All of these things are within Your power, and it is right to bring the common things of our lives to You in prayer. But let us keep sight of the greatest gift You have for us, which is forgiveness of our sins. May we accept that freely offered gift thankfully and remember that nothing else compares to it.*

So, what did it mean to be forgiven of his sins? Well, that, earned through his faith, would have been a ticket to heaven for the paralyzed man. Supposing he never walked again, he had just "won" the greatest prize the universe has to offer.

Then Jesus almost lowers the bar a little, to help those watching (especially the angry Pharisees) understand what He was saying and who He was. He asks which is easier, to say someone is forgiven or to enable a paralyzed man to walk. Of course, viewed through earthly eyes, the latter option would be the most miraculous. So, He heals the paralyzed man.

Those who hadn't understood the magnitude of the first gift could hardly deny the second.

As for the paralyzed man, well, all we know of him after that is that he returned home. But as a man whose faith impressed the Lord, he must have been very aware of the wonderful gifts he had received. No doubt, as a healed paralytic, he did plenty of walking throughout the rest of his life. As a forgiven sinner, he probably combined that walking with a lot of dancing—and praising, too!

THE LITTLE CHILD—
Worth Searching For

At the same time came the disciples unto Jesus, saying, Who is the greatest in the kingdom of heaven? And Jesus called a little child unto him, and set him in the midst of them, and said, Verily I say unto you, Except ye be converted, and become as little children, ye shall not enter into the kingdom of heaven. Whosoever therefore shall humble himself as this little child, the same is greatest in the kingdom of heaven. And whoso shall receive one such little child in my name receiveth me.
MATTHEW 18:1–5 KJV

The disciples, as ordinary men who did not yet fully understand Jesus or His mission, often fell prey to earthly concerns, like which of them would sit at the Lord's right hand in heaven.

To emphasize His message, Jesus brought a child among them and said that one like him would be greater in heaven than all the supposedly great men on earth. Childlike, innocent in love and devotion, without guile or deceit—that was the way to be.

But who was that child? We are never told. We don't know if the child was a boy or a girl. Perhaps it was simply a Galilean child who happened to be nearby. Perhaps it was the child of one of the disciples or another one of Jesus' followers.

Imagine how the parent of the child would have felt (especially if they were a disciple jostling for power in the kingdom to come) to be told that this little one whom they washed, fed, told off occasionally, and who may have spent his days playing in the dirt, would be greater

> Our Father, may we be children of Yours in more than just name, more than just in our prayers and songs. May we search our hearts and find the innocent, kind, loving man or woman You intend us to be. May we trust in You entirely, as every child should trust their father. Amen.

than them in heaven!

How could that possibly be? Perhaps because the disciples had spent longer in the world than the child, they had picked up more bad habits and earthly desires and were further away from God than the little one.

It's an occupational hazard of being alive. Even with the best intentions living this life, we all pick up those habits, and they help chain us to this material world. Jesus' teaching sets us free from those chains and, hopefully, returns us to a more innocent, childlike (but not childish) state. He brings us closer to purity.

As for the little child. . . With such a start to life and such a teacher, it would be no surprise at all to learn that he (or she) played an important role in the church. Perhaps he is even named elsewhere in the Bible as an adult. It matters not. In picking an unnamed child, Jesus set an example and made it plain that He is speaking to the child in every one of us.

THE THREE THOUSAND SOULS—
That's Some Altar Call

Then they that gladly received his word were baptized: and the same day there were
added unto them about three thousand souls. And they continued steadfastly in the
apostles' doctrine and fellowship, and in breaking of bread, and in prayers. And fear
came upon every soul: and many wonders and signs were done by the apostles.
ACTS 2:41–43 KJV

The apostles, full to overflowing with the Holy Spirit, were really shaking things up. This part of the story generally focuses on the wonderful things done to them and through them.

But what about the three thousand who were converted? We never hear about them again. Well, that's the way it is for most of us.

Possibly, some of those supposedly converted were simply in awe of the apostles and wanted to be part of something new and exciting. When the time came to put their new priorities into action, to make a change in their everyday lives once the show was over, a lot of them probably just drifted back to the lifestyle they were familiar with. The same probably happens at modern rallies and altar calls.

But many of them would have been profoundly affected by what they saw and heard. They would have welcomed Jesus into their hearts and been changed in the process.

So, what of them after that?

Dear Lord, I know You know me. I know You value me. I know that even if the rest of the world never hears my name, there will be a particular spot reserved only for me in Your heart. It is enough. I am content.

Well, they probably went to work, cared for their families. . .all the usual things. Sure, they would have a story to tell and perhaps their example would help influence others, but it's wrong to expect them to become the equivalent of first-century rock stars.

The named people we read about in the Bible, the movers and shakers, are all very necessary, but they are the exceptions. They promoted and preserved the faith, sometimes at the cost of their lives (and we are grateful to them), but that's not what the faith is about.

A huge proportion of all the believers who ever lived were like those of the three thousand who stayed converted. They never made headlines, they never shook the establishment; they simply lived godly lives, raised godly children, and tried their best to be the men or women their Creator meant them to be.

It would be nice (I guess) to run a megachurch, to be a spiritual adviser to the people in power, but again, those positions are the exception rather than the rule. If you don't do those things, you needn't think yourself any less than those who do. God doesn't. He could name each of those three thousand converts.

They were the merest sentence in biblical history—but they were the people the Lord was sent to earth to save. As are you.

THE ROYAL OFFICIAL—
Signs and Wonders

When this man heard that Jesus had arrived in Galilee from Judea,
he went to him and begged him to come and heal his son, who was
close to death. "Unless you people see signs and wonders," Jesus told him,
"you will never believe." The royal official said, "Sir, come down before
my child dies." "Go," Jesus replied, "your son will live."
JOHN 4:47–50 NIV

Jesus had gone on a walking tour to avoid the plotting of the Pharisees. He had passed through Samaria (putting that part of the trip to very good use) and eventually arrived at Cana in Galilee.

A royal official, perhaps a member of the court of King Herod, sought Him out begging that He save his dying son.

Perhaps it was weariness from the journey that made the Lord sigh and reply, "Unless you people see signs and wonders you will never believe." Or, perhaps it was because royal officials and nobles of the court would tend to have nothing to do with Him unless there was something in it for them.

Neither of those reasons stopped Jesus from restoring the man's son to full health. If it hadn't exactly been faith that drove the royal official to seek out Jesus, then it had been love for his son, and love and faith are close cousins. When Jesus told

> *Why do we not believe? Well, some wonders and signs are almost too big to see. And our fears blind us to Your work— fear of appearing foolish, fear of losing influence. . . . Lord, help us see that these are only distractions attempting to hide the greatest wonder of all, this creation and Your signature all over it. May we come to You not always in desperation, but more often in admiration as willing worshippers.*

him to go home, the royal official left certain—convinced by the encounter—that his son would be healed. Faith might not have taken him to Jesus, but faith had been the result of the encounter with Him.

When he arrived home, the royal official discovered his son had started to get well at the exact same time Jesus had said, "Your son will live."

And so it is with many.

We believe because we have run out of alternatives. Or we believe after the fact, once we have seen the signs and wonders. Neither of those reasons disqualify our faith. But wouldn't it be better to believe at a time and place where it seems like there is nothing to be gained through it, to come to faith because it seems so right or because it makes our hearts sing?

(Of course, there is always something to be gained through belief in the Lord Jesus Christ. Just not necessarily in this world.)

Perhaps we don't get to choose how and when it happens to us, but the Lord must surely smile when someone becomes a believer willingly, under no duress, and for no other reason than through love.

THE LAME MAN—
Healed at the Beautiful Gate

Then Peter said, "Silver or gold I do not have, but what I do have I give you.
In the name of Jesus Christ of Nazareth, walk." Taking him by the right hand,
he helped him up, and instantly the man's feet and ankles became strong.
He jumped to his feet and began to walk. Then he went with them into
the temple courts, walking and jumping, and praising God.
ACTS 3:6–8 NIV

⸺⸺

He had been lame from birth and may have made a decent enough living begging from visitors to the temple. That he wasn't resigned to the life of a beggar or a cripple is evident by the way he jumped and danced when Peter healed him. He had received a great gift and he knew it!

Peter and John had been walking by when he asked them for money. Peter then braced himself and determined to put his faith into action, performing the kind of miracle he had seen his Master do.

When the man refused to let them go, insisting on going into the temple with them and telling anyone who would listen about the healing, Peter seized the opportunity and gave an epic speech that was heard by many. He and John were jailed for it, but that still counted as a success.

So, what do we learn from the example of the lame man? Well,

> *Dear Lord, not all of us are the "happy clappy" type, completely uninhibited in their love for You. And not all of us are the "prim and proper" type, preferring a more refined and subtle appreciation. Both are great because the world is full of different people who respond to different styles. Help us find our talent, our style, our way of communicating Your love, then watch us preach it in the way we can!*

he didn't just keep quiet about the wonder God worked in his life. He made a real song and dance about it, telling as many people as would listen.

No doubt he was sorry to see his benefactor arrested. He would have been comforted to know that he had played a little part in swelling the numbers of the early Christians. Perhaps he even came to faith himself.

It's one thing to be thankful to God for all the good things He does in your life but keep it to yourself. It's quite another to indulge in such wild celebration that people get arrested. But we have to realize that people are affected; people are brought to faith and salvation through stories such as the one the formerly lame man told. It might be sensible to find a middle way to do it, or a way that suits your particular skills, but if you have a story to tell about how God worked in your life, then you owe it to those who have never encountered Him to tell it.

THE JAILER OF
PAUL AND SILAS—
Wakened in More Ways Than One

And the keeper of the prison awaking out of his sleep, and seeing the
prison doors open, he drew out his sword, and would have killed himself,
supposing that the prisoners had been fled. But Paul cried with a loud voice,
saying, Do thyself no harm: for we are all here. Then he called for a light,
and sprang in, and came trembling, and fell down before Paul and Silas,
and brought them out, and said, Sirs, what must I do to be saved?
ACTS 16:27–30 KJV

⸺ ∽∽∽ ⸺

His first unthinking action was to draw his sword to kill himself. This
was the world he lived and worked in; having failed his masters, it was
better to die by his own hand than face them.

Many nonbelievers live in similar worlds, even today.

He had been tasked with guarding two Christian troublemakers.
But if Paul and Silas were out to cause trouble, it was the likes of
which the jailer had never seen. While he slept, they sang hymns,
knowing the other prisoners were listening. When an earthquake
occurred, either by a force of nature or divine intervention (if there is
any difference), all the prison doors sprang open.

Every experience of his life told the jailer his charges would have
escaped and his life would be forfeit because of it. But, no. Paul calmly reassured him that all his prisoners were still where they ought to be. The jailer's life was restored.

In gratitude he took them to his home, washed

> *Almighty God, there are no cages*
> *in Your creation except the ones*
> *we build and the ones Your*
> *adversary tricks us into believing*
> *exist. Help us walk in freedom*
> *that we might lead the way for*
> *other prisoners to follow. Amen!*

their wounds, fed them, and asked what he must do to become like them.

The jailer must have thought the world he lived in was the only one. When he discovered there was another way—a way that wouldn't force him to take his own life and leave his family uncared for, but would actually provide life everlasting for him and his family—is it any wonder he was overwhelmed? He instantly discarded the rules of the old way, treating his prisoners like brothers and setting them free just as he must have felt that he had been set free.

That life-altering shock is still available.

If you know someone who feels the world is set on grinding them down or someone who treats others badly in accordance with the rules of this world, set them free. You don't have to sit and sing them hymns all night like Paul and Silas did with the jailer. You have to do the other thing they did—behave according to the expectations of the world above rather than this world below. They will come to want what you have. Even jailers recognize freedom when they see it.

THE MASTER OF THE BANQUET—
Unknowingly Drank the Wine of Heaven

Jesus said to the servants, "Fill the jars with water"; so they filled them to the brim. Then he told them, "Now draw some out and take it to the master of the banquet." They did so, and the master of the banquet tasted the water that had been turned into wine. . . . Then he called the bridegroom aside and said, "Everyone brings out the choice wine first and then the cheaper wine after the guests have had too much to drink; but you have saved the best till now."

JOHN 2:7–10 NIV

We don't know who the "master of the banquet" was, but if his role was anything other than that of a visiting dignitary (if he was responsible in any way for the organizing of the banquet), then he did a poor job and Jesus did him a big favor.

A wedding feast running out of wine would have been more than just an embarrassment; it might have become a social stigma that stayed with the couple for years.

Mary seemed to recognize the importance of this when she urged Jesus to help. The first miracle He ever did was to help some newlyweds by turning water into wine.

The master of the feast seemed blissfully unaware of the problem (or the solution), settling for complimenting the groom on the excellent quality of this surprising new wine. He never looked deeper than the surface, never wondered what happened or how. He simply saw a wonderful thing—and drank a toast to it!

His joie de vivre is

> *Perhaps, Lord, we close our eyes to many of Your wonders because they would overwhelm us if we truly understood them. But unfold them gently to us and our understanding—that we might be better prepared for heaven!*

perhaps to be admired. His curiosity. . .not so much! But many people live their lives like that, prepared to accept whatever happens without question. It's a simple approach that no doubt helps them toward a stress-free life. But imagine what he would have found had he dug a little deeper.

Our hearts beat—we know how but don't know why. Cut skin heals by itself—we know how but don't know why. The laws of the universe keep our planet spinning around the life-giving sun. Everything that grows understands the seasons. People's hearts ache for a God some would tell us doesn't exist. Why? Why? Why?

Science does a decent job of explaining how things happen, but it all gets a bit more mysterious when we ask why.

We can live like the master of the banquet if we want a simple, uncomplicated, ultimately meaningless life. But if we prefer a wondrous, beautiful, purposeful existence, we need to look deeper. And, looking closer at the world surrounding us, we can't help but end up—time and again—with the One through whom it was all created, the One the master of the banquet missed—Jesus Christ!

THE UNNAMED DISCIPLE—
On the Road to Emmaus

Now that same day two of them were going to a village called Emmaus,
about seven miles from Jerusalem. They were talking with each other
about everything that had happened. As they talked and discussed
these things with each other, Jesus himself came up and walked along
with them; but they were kept from recognizing him.
LUKE 24:13–16 NIV

By the time of His crucifixion, Jesus' disciples numbered far more than the original twelve. Cleopas, for instance, was not one of the Twelve. Neither was his unnamed traveling companion on the road to Emmaus.

The initial two travelers became three as Jesus joined them (without revealing His true identity at first). Jesus and Cleopas did most of the talking from that point on, so what purpose did the other disciple serve in the story?

Well, he could back Cleopas up when he told the Twelve (now the Eleven after Judas's death) about their encounter with the risen Christ—although Jesus confirmed everything they said pretty effectively by appearing among the group apparently out of nowhere. But the unnamed traveler served another purpose, too.

Faith might be a solitary thing in one way—a relationship between you and God involving no one

Dear Lord, I need no one but You, but a trusted traveling companion through this dangerous world would be nice. Having You walk with me through the faith of another would be a great comfort. If that is not Your will, then may I be the companion and source of Your love for another traveler, bolstering their spirits along the way and helping them reach their heavenly home safely.

else—but living it and exploring it often requires company.

The two disciples were not only a physical comfort for each other in a time when they might have been persecuted, but they were also intellectual and spiritual company. Each man on his own might have had trouble processing all that had just occurred. They had just seen their leader, the Son of God, crucified. The sky had darkened and the earth had shaken! That's the kind of thing that leads to post-traumatic stress disorder. But by talking it out together, they not only confirmed the reality of their experiences, but they may also have come to a deeper understanding of it all. Two heads, as they say, are better than one.

There is a verse from Matthew that says, "For where two or three gather in my name, there I am with them" (18:20 NIV). Cleopas and his anonymous friend found this to be literally the truth.

We are all on a journey through faith. None of us understands it all. Indeed, it is supposed to be beyond understanding—which is why it is important to have a traveling companion (or two or three. . .) to help you along the way.

You can be Cleopas or the unnamed guy. It doesn't matter. God knows who you are. What matters is that you help a friend along the road to Jesus.

THE UNHAPPY BROTHER—
Inspired the Parable of the Rich Fool

Someone in the crowd said to him, "Teacher, tell my brother to divide the
inheritance with me." Jesus replied, "Man, who appointed me a judge or an
arbiter between you?" Then he said to them, "Watch out! Be on your guard
against all kinds of greed; life does not consist in an abundance of possessions."
LUKE 12:13–15 NIV

Some people just do not get it! Or, rather, they *will* not get it. Some folks are just too wrapped up in their petty squabbles to accept a wonderful gift when it is presented to them; the drama of their lives is more important to them than the unfolding of God's plan for the universe.

Jesus had been preaching to thousands of people (so many that they were stepping on each other) about the danger of "him who. . . has authority to throw you into hell" (Luke 12:5), and about promising to speak up for whoever spoke up for Him as well as promising to disown those who were ashamed of Him. He warned against blaspheming the Holy Spirit and advised His listeners on how to speak if they were persecuted.

In the middle of all this important heavyweight instruction, some guy shouted out from the crowd asking the Lord to tell his brother to give him the money he owed him.

Can't you just imagine Jesus sighing? That man's priorities

> *Dear Lord, we can all be fools at times, especially when it comes to what we think we are due. A healthier way might be to realize that we are due nothing, that everything we have is a gift from the One who knows our needs better than anyone. May we pause from time to time and thank You not only for what we have but for what You in Your wisdom have kept from us.*

were instantly, and sadly, apparent. Not family, but money.

Despite the fact that He will eventually advocate for all of us in heaven, Jesus declared that He wasn't sent here to judge those kinds of disputes. He basically told the guy He had more important things to do. But the interruption did inspire the Parable of the Rich Fool, where Jesus told his audience (and millions of people down the generations) that there was no point in being greedy when all you accumulate could be taken away from you—or you from it—at any moment.

Do you think the man in the crowd got the message? Or did he just go home and continue complaining about his brother's greed while turning a blind eye to his own?

So, what are the lessons to be drawn from this unhappy brother? The first is surely that possessions ought to be the least of our worries and that we ought to strive instead to be "rich toward God" (Luke 12:21 NIV).

The other lesson is that when you meet a man famous for His on-the-spot parables, try to make sure He doesn't come up with one about you. Especially not one with "fool" in the title!

THE BLIND MEN OF JERICHO—
They Would Not Be Quiet

Two blind men were sitting by the roadside, and when they heard that Jesus
was going by, they shouted, "Lord, Son of David, have mercy on us!"
The crowd rebuked them and told them to be quiet, but they shouted all the louder,
"Lord, Son of David, have mercy on us!" Jesus stopped and called them.
"What do you want me to do for you?" he asked. "Lord," they answered,
"we want our sight." Jesus had compassion on them and touched their eyes.
Immediately they received their sight and followed him.
MATTHEW 20:30–34 NIV

❧

Asking for help is difficult. Beggars would have to ask—or starve—but because people with disabilities in biblical times had to depend entirely on the kindness of the local population, it was unwise to annoy people.

The two blind beggars of Jericho must have heard many stories about Jesus and the miraculous healings He performed. Whoever told them those stories must have been very convincing.

When they heard He was passing by on His way out of the city, they took what might well have been their last chance and shouted out to Him. The crowd Jesus had attracted locally must have been annoyed at them. Perhaps they thought the beggars were presenting a bad image of their city to this distinguished visitor. Whatever their reasons, they told the blind men to be quiet.

If Jesus had failed to hear them or to heal them, the people telling them to be quiet would be the ones

> *Lord, the voices crying against You, that insist we are foolish for believing in You, are many and almost overwhelming at times. Give us the vision to see that they are strictly temporary while You are eternal!*

providing the alms the next day, and the next day. It is a measure of their faith that the two blind men ignored the protestations and shouted again "all the louder."

If Jesus hadn't heard them, they might well have starved for their efforts. But He did, and He restored their sight. Thereafter they followed Him. Well. . .can you imagine a better use for the gift of sight than looking always at Jesus?

The people who told the beggars to be quiet—who couldn't believe they'd had the nerve to speak to this man, who had no understanding of Him or the faith involved in approaching Him—they have their counterparts in the modern world. Those of us who try to live a life of faith will find various individuals and institutions telling us to be quiet, suggesting that we keep our faith to ourselves.

We need to have the courage of those two blind men. We need to understand that Jesus is our only chance at eternal life. When the voices of this world try to drown Him or us out, we have to shout all the louder.

If along the way we can help some of those shouting against us to "see," then so much the better.

THE TWO PROSTITUTES—
One a Mother, the Other a Liar

Then the king said, "Bring me a sword." So they brought a sword for the king.
He then gave an order: "Cut the living child in two and give half to one and half
to the other." The woman whose son was alive was deeply moved out of love for her
son and said to the king, "Please, my lord, give her the living baby! Don't kill him!"
But the other said, "Neither I nor you shall have him. Cut him in two!"

1 KINGS 3:24–26 NIV

———— ⬤ ————

The first biblical example of Solomon's God-given wisdom involves two women of the lowest social status and no name other than a bad one.

These two prostitutes lived together, worked together, and gave birth at the same time. But during the night, one had rolled over and accidentally smothered her baby. In the morning, rather than being racked by grief—and perhaps trying to protect herself from any blame—she took her companion's living baby and claimed it was hers.

> *Lord, the woman in this story was among the lowest of the low, but love still brought out something beautiful in her—something You placed in her soul at her creation. May we never deem anyone beyond Your redemption or our help. And if there seems to be no love in their lives, may we put some there, trusting it will grow and be transformative. For where love is, You are also.*

Solomon had to decide which of them was lying, but there were no witnesses and only the women's opposing testimonies to go on.

Now, pause and imagine any other land where such a case would have come before the king. In most worldly kingdoms, people of such low class and little financial means could never hope to appeal directly to the king. Apparently they could in Israel. And they certainly can in the kingdom of God. We may not get the answer we desire (and these two women got a ruling that surprised both of them), but every plea for aid and justice will be heard by the Lord above.

When Solomon drew a sword and declared his intention to give each woman half a baby, the true mother rose above her situation and showed that true love is a sacrificial thing. The woman who was not the mother of the living child was content that neither of them would have him. His real mother was prepared to lose her child and see someone else raise him rather than let him come to harm.

God the Father would have understood. His love is also a sacrificial one, sending His Son to die (and rise again) so the rest of us might be redeemed.

As for the woman herself, this may have been the first altruistic thing she had ever done. We can only hope that feeling of sacrificial love bred more of its kind and that she changed her life for the better.

THE SERVANT GIRLS IN THE COURTYARD—
Saying What Peter Didn't Want to Hear

Now Peter was sitting out in the courtyard, and a servant girl came to him.
"You also were with Jesus of Galilee," she said. But he denied it before them all.
"I don't know what you're talking about," he said. Then he went out to the gateway,
where another servant girl saw him and said to the people there, "This fellow was
with Jesus of Nazareth." He denied it again, with an oath: "I don't know the man!"

MATTHEW 26:69–72 NIV

When Jesus was taken before the high priest, beginning the process that would end in crucifixion, Peter, the most assertive and sometimes reckless of all the disciples, followed Him. When the priests began their interrogation, the guards, the servants, and Peter all waited in the shadowy, fire-lit courtyard.

It was a moment filled with high drama and dangerous potential. Peter's courage (which he placed a lot of stock in) was already being put to the test. Jesus had previously predicted that it would fail him, saying Peter would deny his Lord three times. When first one servant girl, then another, and then a man who was standing near him suggested he must have known Jesus, Peter must have been very aware of the nearby guards and his own mortality.

Three times, as Jesus predicted, Peter denied his

> *Almighty God, the things we do in fear will almost always be wrong. If they weren't wrong, we would not fear. When the world heightens our anxieties, help us to look inward—or upward—to see what we ought to do or what You would have us do. Then give us the courage to do it. Once we know we are living in Your will, fear will have no place in our lives.*

Lord to save his own skin.

Jesus would not have said such a thing to mock Peter. God would not have arranged such a situation simply to humiliate him. But Peter was a better servant after his pomposity was pricked. He would become pivotal in the formation of the church and the spreading of the Word, but first he had to get over himself. A man who thought too much of himself would not have been much use in God's plan.

The voices that taunted Peter in the courtyard and stoked his fear might almost be considered evil or satanically directed. Certainly, they seemed intent on putting Peter in harm's way. But the prediction had to come true, the point had to be made, Peter needed to be torn down before he could be built up again.

Sometimes God talks to us or challenges us through the voice of our conscience. In Peter's case, God challenged him through the voices of servant girls and a bystander. No harm resulted and he was a better man for it—eventually.

All too often we are quick to label things as evil when actually they are simply challenging, and it is our responses to them that are in the wrong.

THE WIDOW OF NAIN—
The First Resurrection

Now when he came nigh to the gate of the city, behold, there was a dead man carried out, the only son of his mother, and she was a widow: and much people of the city was with her. And when the Lord saw her, he had compassion on her, and said unto her, Weep not. And he came and touched the bier: and they that bare him stood still. And he said, Young man, I say unto thee, Arise. And he that was dead sat up, and began to speak. And he delivered him to his mother.

LUKE 7:12–15 KJV

In the time of Jesus, people were familiar with "wonder workers." They traveled from town to town attracting crowds, performing tricks, and collecting money for their efforts. Some even claimed to be able to raise the dead!

What made Jesus different? The widow of Nain doubtless told many people what made Him different.

She was at the lowest point of her life. Her husband had died some time previously. Now her son, a young man and the hope for her security in her old age, had also died. Laying aside the pain of the grief and the loss, she now faced destitution. If she survived at all, it would be on the charity of others.

She—like all of us—had nothing to offer Jesus. Nor did He look for anything. His "wonders" were not done for gain, not performed to acquire a reputation for Himself. His miracles were

> *Dear Lord, You are nothing like the world expected. You have no care for name or status, but You care for the lowly, the dispossessed, the grieving, the ones who can offer nothing by way of payment. You offer them—and us—everything in return. If we are slow to comprehend, it is because You are nothing like what the world has ever known. Forgive us. Love us. Amen.*

almost always done out of pity, out of mercy, out of empathy. . .and to enhance only the reputation of God!

When Jesus came upon the funeral cortege, He wasn't upset for the deceased. He was upset for the woman left behind. When He brought the boy back to life—His first recorded resurrection—He didn't tell him to repent or live a good life or spread the word. He presented the son to the mother because His concern was for her.

The widow of Nain was an important part of the healing of the world that continues to this day. Jesus turned the world's priorities upside down, making the least the most important, giving everything to those who had nothing, offering love and life free of cost.

A poor grieving woman was one of the first to receive that gift. What other power would have made her its priority? She was the first but she was far from the last; many more are still to come who will know that kind of love and that kind of new life, freed from death.

THE WOMAN WITH THE ALABASTER BOX—
She Loved Much

And, behold, a woman in the city, which was a sinner, when she knew
that Jesus sat at meat in the Pharisee's house, brought an alabaster box
of ointment, and stood at his feet behind him weeping, and began
to wash his feet with tears, and did wipe them with the hairs of
her head, and kissed his feet, and anointed them with the ointment.

LUKE 7:37–38 KJV

❦

The woman was known by one name before she met Jesus—sinner! Oh, sure, she had an ordinary name, but the priests and the people who lived in the town and the writer of the Gospel of Luke knew her as a sinner. After her encounter with Jesus, she was known in a different way—as one who loved much and had been forgiven much.

The fact that she was there at all tells us something about Jesus' host for the meal. If passersby and people of low class could get so close to his guest, they must have been dining in public. The host was one of the Pharisees, who weren't notable supporters of Jesus' ministry. Perhaps he wanted to show off that such a famous man was dining with him. Perhaps he wanted to embarrass Jesus publicly in theological debate. Whatever his reasons, they distracted him from his duties as host.

What brought this openly sinful woman to the spectacle we can only imagine. Perhaps she simply followed

> Sweet Lord, the beauty and power of Your forgiveness is almost beyond words, almost beyond belief, but we can believe in it because we see it at work in others and we read about it in the Bible stories. May we also believe that it is meant for us in particular, and may we have the courage to step forward and accept it.

the crowd. Or perhaps God arranged for her to be there to take the conceited Pharisee down a peg or two. Or perhaps the goodness that was still in her yearned to be cleansed.

The power of the presence of the Lord obviously affected her deeply. She stepped forward and stood behind His feet in a position of humble service. (Jesus may have been reclining sideways on a low couch or cushions.)

Now, imagine how you would feel being in His presence, knowing that you had no secrets from this Man and that He loved you more than any earthly parent and always had, even when you actively debasing the gift of life He gave you.

It's no surprise that the tears came. It's no surprise that they came in a flood. Years worth of sin were being washed away. A lifetime of despair was being replaced by eternal hope. Those would have been tears of deep regret intermingled with drops of joy.

This unnamed woman is the sinner in all of us who will one day find herself at the feet of the Lord. And she is the promise of forgiveness. All we have to do is step closer to Jesus.

THE PHARISEE—
Look Who Came to Dinner

Then he turned toward the woman and said to Simon, "Do you see this woman?
I came into your house. You did not give me any water for my feet, but she
wet my feet with her tears and wiped them with her hair. You did not give
me a kiss, but this woman, from the time I entered, has not stopped kissing my
feet. You did not put oil on my head, but she has poured perfume on my feet."
LUKE 7:44–46 NIV

With a few notable exceptions, the Pharisees were not fans of Jesus and His work. Those who were impressed sought Him out under the cover of darkness lest their colleagues discovered it. So, for this Pharisee to invite Jesus to dine with him in public he must have been a very loving man—or he had an ulterior motive.

Many times the Pharisees tried to trap Jesus with theological and scriptural arguments. Perhaps this was another such attempt. No doubt this man was very learned and had marshaled all his best arguments and most difficult questions. He probably spent quite some time in study and discussion preparing for the encounter.

So much so that he quite neglected to show his guest much in the way of hospitality (which discounts the possibility that he loved Jesus).

Hospitality, especially among peoples who have little else to offer, is usually a very important part of the culture, with hosts putting their guests before themselves, even to the point of going hungry

> *Father God, it's a simple idea. Too simple, perhaps, for us to get our heads around how powerful it is. If we love, we serve You and the greater good. If we are concerned first and foremost with ourselves, we negate that. May we, in every situation, have the courage and understanding to focus first on loving the person You placed in front of us.*

so that their guests might be fed. The Pharisee was so wrapped up in himself and his own plans that most of the hospitality—the washing of feet, the kiss, the oil for His hair—was left to a passerby. A sinful woman took on the responsibilities of this noble, educated, religious man.

God loves to prick the bubbles of our pomposity.

When we become so engrossed in ourselves, we forget others. And that's not how God's plan works. We are called to be servants for each other, putting our guests and our brothers and sisters first, that way there is no judgment and no hatred. Even in an antagonistic situation like the meeting between this troublesome preacher and this pillar of the establishment, if the host had begun the meeting in love, then perhaps they may have gone on to a better understanding of each other.

But the Pharisee put himself and his party first—then God included the story of his foolishness in the Bible for the world to read.

JAIRUS'S DAUGHTER—
Love in This World,
Hope for the Next

While Jesus was still speaking, someone came from the house of Jairus,
the synagogue leader. "Your daughter is dead," he said.
"Don't bother the teacher anymore." Hearing this, Jesus said to Jairus,
"Don't be afraid; just believe, and she will be healed."

LUKE 8:49–50 NIV

Jesus had just spoken about His own imminent death to the followers of John the Baptist when He heard a child was dying.

The father of that child was a "ruler of the synagogue." As such, he was part of the religious establishment that found Jesus so problematic. But when it came to the life and death of his child, nothing he could offer—even as a man of influence with powerful associates—was of any use.

His beloved child's closeness to death stripped away any pretense and all arrogance. Death and love were the two most real things in his world at that moment, and he badly needed one to overcome the other. He knew—simply knew—there was only one man to turn to. His request to the Lord that He restore his daughter shows what Jairus might have hidden or denied on any other day—absolute belief.

Jesus laid aside all thoughts of His own impending death, healed the bleeding woman along the way, and rushed to restore the twelve-year-old to her family.

> *Beautiful Savior, this world would be a dead-end street without You. We are inexpressibly thankful that You turn it into a highway to glory. May we never be so blinded and diverted by the things of the world that we forget this wonderful fact and lose sight of Your beauty and the salvation that is in Your love.*

We know nothing else about the girl. We can only imagine her life was never the same again. How could she not grow to be a woman of faith and a devout worker for the new church?

But we do know God used her for a purpose. As a child, she was the closest thing to innocence we know in this world. The love her parents felt for her would be the nearest we can come to the love God has for us. Compared with the state our soul yearns to return to and the essential, most elemental force in the universe, everything else we occupy ourselves with in these mortal lives is really unnecessary nonsense.

We build up our careers, our reputations, our power base, our finances, our property portfolios, and they appear to make a difference to our lives. But when faced with the realities of life (and death), none of them can help.

Jairus's unnamed daughter is a symbol, a reminder of what is real and important. She also, through her death and resurrection, points the way to the only One who makes sense of this world, by using it as a gateway to the next—Jesus Christ.

THE ONES WHO LAUGHED—
Nothing Better to Offer

*Meanwhile, all the people were wailing and mourning for her.
"Stop wailing," Jesus said. "She is not dead but asleep." They laughed
at him, knowing that she was dead. But he took her by the hand
and said, "My child, get up!" Her spirit returned, and at once she
stood up. Then Jesus told them to give her something to eat.*
LUKE 8:52–55 NIV

Many cultures have professional mourners who will add to the wailing at a person's death in the hope of a gratuity from the family. Jairus's family had good reason to weep; their beloved twelve-year-old daughter had died. But Jairus was an important man in the community. The ruler of the synagogue would have plenty of people keen to garner favor. Many of those would have made a show of weeping and wailing.

We can be pretty sure it was them and not the girl's family who laughed when Jesus said she was alive!

It's easy to be a mocker. Often it is because of thoughtlessness (or the belief that they are somehow wiser than the hopeful ones) when mockers declare that nothing works, everything's pointless, there is no hope. At its very worst, scoffing is the work of the devil, trying to blind people to the possibility of God.

The mourners at the house of Jairus probably

> Almighty God, the voices of the naysayers are loud and difficult to ignore. Of course, they would not be so loud if there was not so much goodness and positivity for them to overcome. Help us not be disheartened by them. Give us the strength to ignore them—but may we never forget them. They are the proof that Your work is necessary, and they need You more than most.

felt that Jesus was spoiling their day. They were women of the world; they knew about girls and health and dying. They could have told Him a thing or two. In their minds, they were probably already planning the meal afterward and whom they would tell about everything that happened. Perhaps they were watching each other, thinking this one wasn't putting her heart into it, or that one was overdoing it. Jairus, despite how cynical he may have been about Jesus before, at least reached out positively.

Jesus walked past the pretense of the women and restored the girl, making their phony grief redundant. But before they had to face the facts, their initial response was to mock Him as a fool.

Even these days, people will be quick to mock a fool. But in their minds the term "fool" includes optimists, believers, and people who try to make the world a better place. As difficult as it can be, we mustn't respond to them in anger or hide away from them in hurt. We should do what Jesus did—walk on past them and prove them wrong.

Then we might pity them and show them a better way. After all, they are the ones who are really being fooled.

BELSHAZZAR'S MOTHER—
The Wisdom of Old

Now the queen by reason of the words of the king and his lords came into the
banquet house: and the queen spake and said, O king, live for ever: let not thy
thoughts trouble thee, nor let thy countenance be changed: There is a man in thy
kingdom, in whom is the spirit of the holy gods; and in the days of thy father
light and understanding and wisdom, like the wisdom of the gods, was found in
him; whom the king Nebuchadnezzar thy father, the king, I say, thy father,
made master of the magicians, astrologers, Chaldeans, and soothsayers.

DANIEL 5:10–11 KJV

———∞∞∞———

Belshazzar was not the man his father was.

As a great and powerful king, Nebuchadnezzar had thought
himself more important than God, so God humbled him until he
realized that all he held was a gift from heaven. As the captor of
the hostage Israelites, Nebuchadnezzar tried to assimilate them into
his own people before Daniel showed him the folly of this endeavor.

Daniel and Nebuchadnezzar became a strong team with mutual respect. Nebuchadnezzar's son and heir, Belshazzar, seemed to have forgotten all of that—even forgetting Daniel. He seemed set to repeat his father's youthful arrogance—and did, when he went too far by including the holy vessels of the Hebrew temple

> *Almighty Father, the generations improve but slowly. And some would say they do not improve at all. They need men and women of God to guide them, to make sure that each generation learns from the past and builds upon the experience. May we be those men and women in our own families and communities, but if we cannot be, for whatever reason, then may we always be prepared to point our children toward the ones who are—and to You!*

in a drunken debauch.

The hand of God wrote Belshazzar's fate on the wall in front of all his guests—and it was not good news! Belshazzar was visibly shaken. No one knew what to do.

Into this scene of chaos and fear walked Belshazzar's mother. As widow of Nebuchadnezzar, she remembered the lessons learned in the past, and so she reminded her son that a man of God, honored by his own father, still lived in the kingdom.

God's plan is not that Daniel would put things right for Belshazzar, but that Belshazzar would restore Daniel to a position to later influence Darius the Mede (who kills Belshazzar that same night). Perhaps if Belshazzar's mother had introduced him to the man of God a little earlier, his fate might have been a happier one.

Belshazzar's mother reminds those of us who have learned great lessons—from our own lives, from the lessons in the Bible, and from the lives of the martyrs in the past—how important it is not to keep that knowledge to ourselves. If each new generation is to avoid having to learn from the same mistakes the previous one made, then someone has to teach them. And teach them early, if possible.

PETER'S WIFE—
Invisibly Wonderful

Don't we have the right to food and drink?
Don't we have the right to take a believing wife along with us,
as do the other apostles and the Lord's brothers and Cephas?
1 CORINTHIANS 9:4–5 NIV

———

We have no way of knowing how many of the disciples were married. In most cases, we don't know whether they abandoned those families for the mission or took them along on their travels.

The Bible does refer to Peter's mother-in-law (when Jesus heals her), and in 1 Corinthians Paul refers to apostles such as Cephas (Peter) taking their wives with them on their journeys. So, we can reasonably assume that Peter had a wife.

But what can we suppose about her life?

It would have been a tumultuous one! She would have married Peter when he was an impetuous young fisherman. She could never have imagined that their lives would exceed the confines of their village and the lake. They may well have had children together.

As a man of high and changeable passions, Peter would have been the kind of husband that benefited from a patient and resilient wife.

And then Jesus arrived and everything changed!

He came to their

Father God, who made men and women to be together, drawing strength and security from each other, help us understand and fulfill the roles involved. Let us not be distracted by modern trends and fleeting fashions, but let us bring the true and essential attributes of the male and the female together to form one glorious unit, existing only to sing the praises of the One who made us perfect for each other.

house. He associated closely with her husband. She must have met Him. Did she also become a convert? It is difficult to imagine Peter going on long missions with a wife who didn't at least share this passion.

She would have seen her husband mature, comforted him in his grief, calmed him in his excitement, and watched him become an orator, a leader, an encourager. Such men are impressive in public, but they show their doubts and fears in the safety of the home. There may have been many times when she and her faith gave her husband the courage to go on.

Legend has it that they grew old together and were martyred together in Rome. Supposedly, Peter's last words to her were, "Remember the Lord."

Can there be many things more beautiful than a husband and wife living the life of faith and traveling to glory together?

The phrase "Behind every great man is a great woman" is sometimes seen as a condescending one, but the shadow of a great man is not an easy or comfortable place to stand in. The woman often sees his flaws, his fears, the cracks in the facade, and patches them up with her love. There is no doubt Peter was a great (and flawed) man. It's no great leap to suppose the woman who traveled the many difficult roads with him was also a great wife.

EZEKIEL'S WIFE—
The Innocent Sacrifice

The word of the LORD came to me: "Son of man,
with one blow I am about to take away from you the
delight of your eyes. Yet do not lament or weep or shed any tears."
EZEKIEL 24:15–16 NIV

———

God killed Ezekiel's wife. She was a good woman and He killed her. Where's the justice in that? Where's the love? How could He be so cruel?

God had run out of patience with Israel. Time and again He had delivered them from their trials only to have them turn away and worship false gods. If they wouldn't learn from those times, then perhaps a harsher lesson might get their attention. So, God lined the Assyrians along Israel's border. The invading army would scour the Holy Land and carry its people off in captivity. Many would suffer and die in the process. But many had already suffered and died in sin because of the chosen people's ungodly behavior. Innocents had suffered.

To demonstrate this, God took an innocent—the wife of his most loyal subject, Ezekiel.

He knew Ezekiel would suffer. His wife was, after all, the delight of his eyes. But God instructed him not to be seen grieving. He was to be the example by which the faithful would get through the coming storm. They were to be brave, bear their pains and stay upright, and have faith that God would restore them and that things would be better afterward. They were to set

Almighty Creator, beloved Father, it is for You to give and take. Our role is to understand if we can, but to trust and love You regardless. See us all safely to the great reunion and the better times in heaven.

the example to the unbelievers, the ones who had brought this destruction on the land.

But. . .poor Ezekiel. Or it would have been "poor Ezekiel" if his love for God hadn't been what it was. That higher love saw him through the nights of tears and the desolate days. He was a man of duty; God had explained what it was and given him the strength to carry it out.

Harsh? But what about the promised better times? Though the longest life comes to an end, heaven is forever. The most painful of lives will soon be forgotten in an eternity of love and worship. Ezekiel walked a hard walk but was rewarded for it. Israel suffered but was restored.

His beloved wife was a perfect example of how the godless— claiming they hurt no one but themselves—actually hurt countless innocents in the pursuit of their self-gratification. Had she been asked, she might well have agreed it was a point worth making.

God took her "with one blow" or "immediately." She went from Ezekiel's side to God's side in the blink of an eye. Could a faithful wife ask for any more? And, of course, she was there to welcome Ezekiel home forever and ever when he reached the end of his journey without her.

THE DAUGHTERS OF SHALLUM—
Building a Wall Together

And next unto him repaired Shallum the son of Halohesh,
the ruler of the half part of Jerusalem, he and his daughters.
NEHEMIAH 3:12 KJV

Nehemiah's mission was to rebuild the walls of Jerusalem before the enemies saw what he was doing and attacked to tear them down again. The stones of the old wall were still to hand, but many willing laborers were needed to build them back up again. Nehemiah lists the individuals and families who took part. It's an almost exclusively male list, and in that company, the daughters of Shallum stand out.

Not only because even in safer times such work would have been considered unsuitable for young women, they also stood out because they were the daughters of Shallum, ruler of half of Jerusalem. His apparent humility in working alongside them seems to have been good for his daughters. Had they been the children of another man, they might have claimed they were "too good" for this sort of thing. They might have sent servants.

But they worked in person because the work was necessary.

No doubt they suffered, but there is no record of their shirking. They were working for their own security and for God's glory, which, to any person of faith, ought to be the same thing.

It's a good but painful truth, Lord, that most of the trials in our lives are sent by You for our own good. May we embrace them with enthusiasm, seeing Your wisdom in them, and emerge on the other side, closer to being the men and women You would have us be.

God will often place unexpected situations before us. Too often we look at them and say, "Surely this isn't for us." We find excuses to walk away, convincing ourselves that someone else should deal with it. If Shallum and his daughters had thought that way, there would have been a gap in the city walls when the enemy arrived. Or the whole wall would have been shorter as others left their own work to fill the gap they left.

If God puts the situation in front of us, He means for us to deal with it. If we have "reasons" why we shouldn't, we often find that those reasons are the very issue God is addressing. If we are too weak for the task, the task will make us stronger. If we do not have the understanding for the task, the task itself will increase our understanding.

The young women probably never believed they could build a wall, but they did, and slept all the more securely afterward because of it. Who knows what achievements that experience led to throughout the rest of their lives?

It is not for us to question why God asks these things of us. We need to trust that He has a good reason. Then we need to do as the anonymous daughters of Shallum did—roll up our sleeves and get to work.

JONAH'S MARINERS—
Rowing for Tarshish and Crying to Their Gods

Then the mariners were afraid, and cried every man unto his god, and cast
forth the wares that were in the ship into the sea, to lighten it of them.
But Jonah was gone down into the sides of the ship; and he lay, and was fast asleep.
So the shipmaster came to him, and said unto him, What meanest thou,
O sleeper? arise, call upon thy God, if so be that God will
think upon us, that we perish not.
JONAH 1:5–6 KJV

⸻

These guys were just doing their jobs, going about their business. . .
and hedging their bets.

Faith seems to have been a matter of expediency with them.
They followed no particular god, but in true maritime style, they
cast their net wide, each of them worshipping their own deity in
times of trouble (and probably at no other time).

When the storm hit and the ship was in danger of going down,
the shipmaster even wakened their passenger and told him to get
praying, just in case his god was the one who could help in this particular situation.

God—the real deal—had come crashing into their lives, and as much as they might have been prepared for many different emergencies, they weren't prepared for Him.

As surprising as it might seem, it is entirely possible that Jonah—who was hiding

> *Almighty God, I might not be all that I will one day become, but I am what I am and the best of me is my love for You. May it shine out even in the darkest of times. Flawed as I am, may I be allowed to carry enough of Your love with me to help those who have yet to encounter the You that I know and trust forever.*

from God—was the first representative of the Creator they had ever met.

They were decent men. They didn't treat Jonah harshly even after he revealed himself as the cause of their troubles. When he told them to throw him overboard, they chose instead to row all the harder for the coast. It was only at his insistence—and with terrified pleas to this "new" God—that they finally did as he told them to.

We hear nothing more about them, but we have to assume they made it to Tarshish (thought to be Cádiz in Spain) safely. What a story they would have to tell! A god that took a personal interest! Flawed followers who still had an intimate relationship! Self-sacrifice for the sake of others!

Meeting Jonah would have had a big effect on them. Sure, he was running away from God, but his faith in God and God's abilities came with him.

Even today we may meet people on our journeys who have no clear understanding of who God is. Our lives might not be the best advertisement for Him, but we mustn't let that obscure our belief and our trust.

THE WIDOW OF ZAREPHATH—
Dying to Help

So he went to Zarephath. When he came to the town gate, a widow was there
gathering sticks. He called to her and asked, "Would you bring me a little water
in a jar so I may have a drink?" As she was going to get it, he called,
"And bring me, please, a piece of bread."

1 KINGS 17:10–11 NIV

Queen Jezebel did not appreciate the prophet Elijah's assessment of her character. He became a hunted outcast living in the desert, being fed by birds just to stay alive.

At one point God told him it was time to move on. He had arranged for a widow to take care of the prophet. God may have "arranged" it, but it didn't seem that He told the widow about it. She would have had to come into the situation through an amazing act of faith.

Times were usually difficult for widows in those days, but a drought had made the situation especially difficult. Crops had failed, and the widow and her young son were slowly starving to death. When a stranger—Elijah—approaches asking for water, she interrupts the preparation of their last meager meal to give him a drink.

When he also asks for food, she tells him that they have so little food of their own that after this last meal she was sure she and her son would die.

> Lord above, testing times strengthen us, feeding others nourishes us, strangers usually have a message for us that we need only decipher. If we believe them, we believe everything is in Your hands, including us. What good is life if we live it contrary to the laws of love? May we always share with our brothers and sisters, and may we always see the stranger as one of those brothers or sisters.

Then Elijah does an incredible thing. He asks her to bake him some bread first! Not very sympathetic of him, but, amazingly, she does so—because this man she has never met assures her that God will supply her needs. She feeds the stranger—and God takes care of them all for the next year, ensuring her flour pot and oil jug never run empty.

Our faith expects us to show hospitality to strangers "for by so doing some people have shown hospitality to angels" (Hebrews 13:2 NIV). That's okay in times of plenty, but how about when the going is tougher, when what they need is all you have? That's when faith in the Lord's provision becomes a little more difficult. But those strangers are never strangers to Him. He loves all of us and wants us to help each other. Just as He helps us.

The unnamed widow lived in a heathen land, but her faith in the Great Provider was such that she risked death to do His will. Perhaps she thought, *Either He will save me—or He will take me home and I will never have to worry or go hungry again.* For the truly faithful, it's a win-win situation.

THE MOTHER OF MOSES—
Gave Him Away Twice to Save Him

Now a man of the tribe of Levi married a Levite woman, and she became
pregnant and gave birth to a son. When she saw that he was a fine child,
she hid him for three months. But when she could hide him no longer,
she got a papyrus basket for him and coated it with tar and pitch. Then she
placed the child in it and put it among the reeds along the bank of the Nile.

EXODUS 2:1–3 NIV

※

Moses is remembered as one of the most powerful and influential men of the Old Testament. He not only walked with God, but occasionally changed His mind. But there was a time when he was defenseless and totally dependent on love and kindness.

During the time of Joseph, the Hebrews lived comfortably in Egypt, but a new pharaoh brought new ideas and the Egyptians began to fear the growing number of Hebrews. A decree was issued, stating that newborn Hebrew boys should be killed.

Around that time, a Levite woman married a Levite man and nature took its course. Those nine months must have been a dreadful time for the mother-to-be. If her child was a girl, it would be allowed to live. If it was a boy, it would be put to death.

When she discovered her baby was a boy, she hid him. For three months, both their lives were in danger. Then, when he could be hidden no more, she left him in a basket among the rushes of the Nile. Perhaps she intended

> *Dear Lord, there are powers in this world that may influence our lives and our deaths (if You allow them), but our hearts are Yours alone to influence. While we are in this world, may our actions—however small they might appear—always be noble, always be loving, and always be guided by Your example. We leave the rest up to You.*

that Pharaoh's daughter would find him there, or perhaps she was entrusting him to God.

With a little help from Miriam, Moses' older sister, Moses was found by the daughter of the Pharaoh and his natural mother became his nurse. Eventually, she had to give her son up a second time when Pharaoh's daughter adopted him and named him.

For being a woman of no resources other than those that came naturally, she did incredibly well in a dangerous situation.

We often think of history being played out by men and great powers, but sometimes "weak" things like love and maternal instincts can play a more powerful role than anyone would expect.

Because of the love of one woman for one man, the love of a mother for a child, the love of a sister, and the tenderness of a young princess, Jewish history was changed irrevocably.

Never disparage the "softer" attributes. They have more of an effect than anyone will ever comprehend. Never forget, God is the greatest power in the universe. And God is love!

NOAH'S DAUGHTERS-IN-LAW—
Mothers to Most of Us

In the six hundredth year of Noah's life, on the seventeenth day of the second month—on that day all the springs of the great deep burst forth, and the floodgates of the heavens were opened. And rain fell on the earth forty days and forty nights. On that very day Noah and his sons, Shem, Ham and Japheth, together with his wife and the wives of his three sons, entered the ark.

GENESIS 7:11–13 NIV

The wives of Noah's sons are never named, but they are among the most important women in the Bible, playing a role that only Noah's wife and Eve would understand.

We assume they must have been virtuous God-loving women or the sons of the man chosen to restart the human race would never have chosen them as wives. How they felt going into the ark—leaving the world, family, and friends they had known all their lives behind—we can only imagine. But even more daunting than the thought of what they were leaving behind would have been the thought of what they were about to begin when they touched down on dry land again.

God blessed Noah's sons, telling them to "be fruitful and increase in number and fill the earth" (Genesis 9:1 NIV). But the wives would have the difficult share of that deal. Descendants of Eve, they would become the new mothers of humanity. Each one of us alive today should be

> *Almighty God, we cannot begin to comprehend what our ancestors went through to get us this far. We can thank them best by striving always to grow closer to their God and ours. You give us more chances than we deserve, and we should do our best not to abuse that wonderful privilege. It's what our mothers-after-the-flood would have wanted.*

able to call them Great-great-great-great-great. . .Grandmother.

What gave them the strength to do that? Their relationship with the Almighty. Any doubts they might have had would have been washed away with the flood. We can be sure these were among the most faithful godly mothers ever. Their children would have been raised in the purest of faith.

Through them, God gave mankind a second chance, and they played their part perfectly.

Those second chances weren't reserved for the wives of Shem, Ham, and Japheth. God offers us the opportunity to start over with each new day or, indeed, each new moment. We can leave our broken pasts behind with the help of Jesus and be restored as the human race was.

Of course, the fix wasn't a one-off. After many generations, mankind seemed far enough from God that they would consider building a towel in Babel that would reach heaven and make a name for them.

Our fresh starts often meet the same fate—which is why we should be grateful that God's mercy is beyond our comprehension and the number of new starts we are allowed in this life is limitless.

JOHN THE BAPTIST'S EXECUTIONER— A Life in the Dark

On Herod's birthday the daughter of Herodias danced for the guests and pleased Herod so much that he promised with an oath to give her whatever she asked. Prompted by her mother, she said, "Give me here on a platter the head of John the Baptist." The king was distressed, but because of his oaths and his dinner guests, he ordered that her request be granted and had John beheaded in the prison.

MATTHEW 14:6–10 NIV

What do we know about John the Baptist's executioner? Only that he killed a messenger of God—and he dispatched that duty quickly, leaving time for only the minimum of thought. John the Baptist was probably only one of many who met their end at Herod's whim and this man's blade.

The executioner was probably one of those men content to play a minimal role in his own life, doing whatever those in power asked from him, assuming the responsibility would also be taken by those giving the orders.

Father God, there are no places in this world or in people's minds that Your love and light cannot reach. We ask that You shine in the dark places we might hide from the world and allow us to bear that light and Your Word to others who may be prisoners— willingly or otherwise— of the darkness. Amen!

People like him operate in dark places—like the dungeons of Herod's palace—and keep their consciences locked in dark rooms of their minds. You don't have to be a biblical lackey to live like that. Plenty of people in the modern world would recognize the approach.

The shock of their lives— and afterlives—would come when they faced their Maker and realized that no one else was carrying the can for the things they did and the way they lived their lives. It's a situation each of us will face. Fortunately, we have the life of Jesus and the Bible to prepare us for that moment. We can't claim ignorance—which would be no defense anyway.

The executioner might not have had the Bible, but he had John the Baptist right there in front of him. And John wasn't going anywhere. Popular tradition has Herod visiting John in prison because he liked to listen to him talk (not that he took any of his words seriously). It might have benefited the executioner to sit and listen to John awhile.

John the Baptist, even in chains, was the possibility of God shining a light into the dark places of this man's life. God gives everyone the chance to hear His message. John spoke it. Jesus lived it. You and I might be the ones who deliver it into someone else's dark life.

Because there are no excuses for the follower of God. John may have been in chains, the executioner may have wielded the sword thinking he had all the power. But, really, John was the free man and the executioner was the voluntary prisoner.

THE MAN OF GOD—
A Role for Many to Fill

When King Jeroboam heard what the man of God cried out against the altar
at Bethel, he stretched out his hand from the altar and said, "Seize him!"
But the hand he stretched out toward the man shriveled up, so that he could
not pull it back. Also, the altar was split apart and its ashes poured out
according to the sign given by the man of God by the word of the LORD.

1 KINGS 13:4–5 NIV

Several named people in the Bible are given the title "man of God" because of their great faith. But three times in the Old Testament, someone called only "the man of God" turned up and reminded the ruling powers of their duties to the Lord.

In 1 Samuel, the man of God appeared at the tabernacle and warned the high priest, Eli, that his sons were profaning the Lord's house. He predicted that the outcome of their actions would be death and destitution for the whole family.

He popped up again in 1 Kings where he warned Jeroboam about his family's future desecration of the temple. Jeroboam reached out a hand to him and God caused it to wither. This incarnation of the man of God met a strange end. He was lied to by a prophet and tricked into going against God's instructions. The inevitable result of this was death—by lion attack in this case. But, strangely, the lion did not devour him.

> *Dear Lord, the world sorely needs more men and women with faith enough to make a difference. But such things have become socially unpopular, and the results are plain to see. Should You not raise us up to confront the rulers then at least give us the courage to be men and women of God in our own homes and communities. Amen.*

In 2 Chronicles, King Amaziah was about to go into battle with an army comprised partly of mercenary men from the house of Ephraim. The man of God warned Amaziah that the Lord was not with Israel that day and he should send the Ephraimites home.

It is entirely possible (as all things are possible for God) that these were three incarnations of some heavenly messenger. But it is also possible that they were simply three faith-filled individuals, ordinary men of no other note, whose love of the Lord gave them the confidence to tell the rulers of the land when they were deviating from His plan.

If this important role was played by ordinary men, then it still could be. Imagine the surprise on the faces of the powers that be if they were confronted by an ordinary man or woman with a message directly from God.

Some leaders of religious organizations do attempt to fill that role. But the title of man of God or woman of God is one that any one of us might claim—if we have faith enough, and if God tells us to!

THE GOOD THIEF—
In Paradise with the Lord

And one of the malefactors which were hanged railed on him, saying,
If thou be Christ, save thyself and us. But the other answering rebuked him,
saying, Dost not thou fear God, seeing thou art in the same condemnation?
And we indeed justly; for we receive the due reward of our deeds:
but this man hath done nothing amiss. And he said unto Jesus, Lord,
remember me when thou comest into thy kingdom.

LUKE 23:39–42 KJV

Crucifixion at this time in Israel was almost an industrial process. Jesus as a "failed messiah" did not merit the efforts of the squad of soldiers on His own. He was crucified with at least two other men.

What their crimes were is open for discussion. What isn't in doubt is that they were guilty, and unashamedly so.

One of the men, a sorry lost soul, chose to use his last moments in this world mocking the man dying next to him. The other man had a bit more pity in his heart. He seemed to have at least heard about Jesus. What he heard must have been pretty convincing. He rebuked his companion and addressed Jesus as Lord. Perhaps he felt he had nothing to lose at that point, but his words rang with sincerity and, in fact, he had everything to gain.

In his last moments he turned from his companion in crime, showed mercy, and acknowledged Jesus as the

> *Awesome, beautiful Savior, even in Your agony You would not lose one who may have been counted among the worst of us. What wonderful hope that gives to the rest of us! You truly love us and want to be with us all in heaven forever. May we never imagine we are so far gone that You will not reach out to us, and may we, in turn, invite as many people to paradise as possible.*

only One who could save him. Jesus did not miss that last opportunity to save a soul.

This unnamed thief/malefactor/brigand gets to enter paradise alongside the Lord. What an honor. Did he deserve it? Would any of us have deserved it more?

Supposing he had spent his life robbing, assaulting, even killing people, the love of God is such that, if he really repented, if he truly accepted Jesus, he would be forgiven and welcomed home as a lost lamb.

Exactly the same would apply to any one of us, even supposing our sins were counted much less evil by worldly standards. It's not the sin that's important; it's the saving from sin that matters.

The "good thief" teaches us that there is no depth of depravity we cannot be lifted out of, no place or time in our lives that redemption cannot reach. We might not decide to leave it as late as he did before calling on the Lord, though. His time of death was pretty much fixed. As for the rest of us. . .better not to take the chance. Reach out to Jesus today!

THE MAN WHO DID
NOT KILL ABSALOM—
He Hid Nothing from His King

And Absalom met the servants of David. And Absalom rode upon a mule,
and the mule went under the thick boughs of a great oak, and his head
caught hold of the oak, and he was taken up between the heaven and the earth;
and the mule that was under him went away. And a certain man saw it,
and told Joab, and said, Behold, I saw Absalom hanged in an oak.

2 SAMUEL 18:9–10 KJV

———

Absalom killed his half brother and rebelled against his father, the king. Understanding the grief and rage that drove his son—and knowing how easy it was to fall into sin himself—King David forbade his men from harming his rebel son.

But Absalom was killed anyway. While Absalom dangled from a tree, trapped by his long hair, Joab, David's general, made sure of it, piercing the young prince's heart with three darts. There would be no reconciliation between father and son.

But there was also a man who saw Absalom hanging there and did not kill him. Remembered as "a certain man" in the Bible, he was certain of what he saw and certain of what should be done. It was he who told Joab where Absalom was hanging and he who reminded the powerful older soldier of the king's instructions regarding his son.

Joab demanded to know why the man hadn't slain Absalom there and then, telling him he would have been rewarded if he had. But the certain man

> *Almighty God, how could You not see everything? The universe was made through You and by You. You are in everything and surrounding everything. You know the breaths we take and the beats of our hearts. May we remember this in all our decisions.*

held his ground, insisting there was nothing hidden from the king and if he had disobeyed orders, the same man who was now angry with him for not killing the young prince would, in all likelihood, have hunted him down.

He was between the proverbial rock and a hard place. David and Joab were two very powerful men who wanted very different things. But one was the king to whom the certain man had sworn loyalty and the other was not.

As Christians, we often face similar difficult (if not quite so deadly) decisions. We declare our loyalty to God, but the world is also a powerful force and the two seldom require the same thing of us.

If the certain man thought nothing would escape King David's attention, how much more must we be convinced that nothing we do will escape God's attention? We will have to answer for our actions, so it's best to make as many of them as possible that we would be pleased to hear brought up again in the retelling of our lives.

The certain man was almost certainly prepared to die for his oath and his honor. Let us be "certain" men and women who are prepared to live for ours.

THE BOY OF FIRE AND WATER—
Mustard Seed Faith

A man in the crowd called out, "Teacher, I beg you to look at my son,
for he is my only child. A spirit seizes him and he suddenly screams;
it throws him into convulsions so that he foams at the mouth. It scarcely
ever leaves him and is destroying him. I begged your disciples to drive it out,
but they could not." "You unbelieving and perverse generation," Jesus replied,
"how long shall I stay with you and put up with you? Bring your son here."
LUKE 9:38–41 NIV

Imagine how distraught the father must have been. The "demon" that had power over his son was slowly but surely killing him. He had asked everyone else for help, even the disciples. There was no one else left—except Jesus. And yet again, Jesus was the cure.

He uses the occasion to rebuke the disciples, suggesting that they had better up their game before He leaves.

These days we might think that the boy was suffering from epileptic seizures. It is interesting to think that Jesus suggests enough real faith can cure such maladies.

Regardless of whether this poor child was demon possessed or medically ill, the effects, both on him and the onlookers, would have been the same—sudden injury and shocked horror. Now imagine how it felt for the boy. He would have been doing his best to live an ordinary life but every few minutes, forces he had no control over would throw him this way and that.

The life of faith can be similar. We set out with the best

> Lord, we are still only beginning to understand the power of prayer. Increase, we beg You, the faith in our hearts that we might fully explore this wonderful gift You have given to us. May we begin to move mountains in Your blessed name.

of intentions but forces we can't seem to control soon divert us this way or distract us that way. Our love of God and best intentions are sidelined. We hate it. But it keeps happening. It's not as dramatic as being thrown in the fire or falling into the water, but it can be just as damaging to our spiritual lives.

It's all very well to say that we do have control over how many times we let ourselves down, but those times still keep happening. The devil is insidious. Sometimes he will seduce us into making the wrong decisions. Sometimes he will actually make those decisions and convince us it was our choice—with the resultant loss of self-respect.

We might turn to the modern day equivalent of the disciples—our church elders. If they have faith larger than a mustard seed, they will surely be able to help. But before then, after then, and always, whenever those "seizures" come upon us, we can turn to the source of our strength and the ultimate healer, the One who saved the boy of fire and water—Jesus Christ.

THE SAMARITAN VILLAGERS—
Opposing Heaven for Earthly Reasons

And he sent messengers on ahead, who went into a Samaritan village to get things ready for him; but the people there did not welcome him, because he was heading for Jerusalem. When the disciples James and John saw this, they asked, "Lord, do you want us to call fire down from heaven to destroy them?" But Jesus turned and rebuked them. Then he and his disciples went to another village.

LUKE 9:52–56 NIV

Jesus was literally a man on a mission. The time of His death was approaching and He needed to get to Jerusalem. It's understandable that He didn't have much time for pettiness.

He had already spread the good news among the Samaritans, but this one village obviously thought they had more important things to consider. We aren't told why the villagers refused hospitality to the Lord. But we know they didn't like His destination—Jerusalem. The Jews worshipped at the temple in the Holy City; the Samaritans, who no doubt considered themselves the true inheritors of the Hebrew faith, thought worshipping in Jerusalem was blasphemy. They worshipped on Mount Gerizim since they believed it was where Abraham almost sacrificed Isaac.

Could it be that their annoyance with (or jealousy of) Jerusalem extended to refusing to help travelers trying to get there?

We might laugh at such

> *Dear Lord, it is a simple mission. Not an easy one, but a simple one. We overcomplicate it through our needs, fears, and insecurities. Help us simplify our faith so we may be closer to You and the disciples You sent out on missions with nothing but the clothes they were wearing. May we recognize (and love) Your children through their works and faith, no matter where or how they worship.*

childish obstinacy. But, before we do, we ought to search our own hearts for the things we hold dearer than service to God. How could good Christian people behave like that? Well, ask yourself why there are so many different denominations in the church. Each one of them would have come about because they held a particular interpretation or practice to be more important than the church they split from did.

Fortunately, the denominations coexist well for the most part, but there are some out there who will not speak to or serve with the others. The Samaritan villagers would have understood that mind-set very well.

And what does Jesus think of those deeply held passions? Well, He probably treats them like He did the Samaritan village that He hoped would help Him. He walked around it and left it behind. He had more important things to focus on.

So should we. The purpose of our faith is not to worship an interpretation or a ritual; it is to love God and each other, paying special attention to widows, orphans, the hungry. . .

If we do those things, we will be walking to Jerusalem with the Lord. If not, He might be walking around us so He can do what we've neglected.

THE MAN WHO WOULD FOLLOW JESUS ANYWHERE—
But Did He?

*And it came to pass, that, as they went in the way, a certain man
said unto him, Lord, I will follow thee whithersoever thou goest.
And Jesus said unto him, Foxes have holes, and birds of the air
have nests; but the Son of man hath not where to lay his head.*
LUKE 9:57–58 KJV

⸺∞⸺

We don't know who this man was. He isn't named in the Bible. But many of us will have echoed his enthusiastic outburst. Which of us, when asked, would say anything other than that we would follow Jesus anywhere?

It's easy enough to say, but Jesus went to some pretty unpleasant places. And following Him meant leaving behind a lot of things most people are attached to—like their bed, possessions, and a lot of their preconceptions.

So, did the man live up to his promise? It would be nice to think he became a follower, perhaps one of the seventy-two disciples sent out on missions, perhaps appearing later in the story as a named individual, but. . .

He is listed among three similar "enthusiasts" used to indicate that the cost of following the Lord was more than most expected. One asks leave to say good-bye to his family. Jesus tells him there is no point in beginning if he is going

> *Sweet Jesus, beloved Savior, we are not the followers You deserve, and we could never hope to be. But we could do more. May we surround ourselves with opportunities to ignite our enthusiasm, and may You encourage the flame to burn ever brighter so we might have the courage to follow where You lead more and more often until we are truly living the life You planned for us.*

to turn back so soon. The other asks leave to bury his dead father. Jesus says His concern is with the living.

The man who proclaimed he will follow the Lord "whithersoever thou goest" (or "anywhere") was reminded that this meant having no home but heaven, no family but God and God's children, and no place to rest his head because there would be very little rest.

It's a big cost. Like most, he probably didn't follow through on his promise. What would this world be like if more of us did? Transformed is what it would be.

Perhaps we can forgive this unknown fellow his well-meaning enthusiasm. Jesus was there in front of him with many miraculous deeds and great promises to His name. Some of us get as excited at much lesser things, like a really good sermon or a praise concert.

We shouldn't disparage that enthusiasm. But neither should we let it fade away after the concert is over or once we leave church and step back into the "real" world.

What a follower that man might have made if only he had kept that passionate flame burning. What a difference we might make for the Lord if only we could do the same!

THE MAN BY THE
POOL OF BETHESDA—
Helped in an Unexpected Way

In these lay a great multitude of impotent folk, of blind, halt, withered,
waiting for the moving of the water. For an angel went down at a certain
season into the pool, and troubled the water: whosoever then first after the
troubling of the water stepped in was made whole of whatsoever disease he had.
And a certain man was there, which had an infirmity thirty and eight years.
JOHN 5:3–5 KJV

The healing abilities of the Bethesda pool were a long-established tradition. They weren't thought of as a superstition. Indeed, they had angelic—and therefore heavenly—associations. They were an accepted way of getting healed from all kinds of ailments—but only if you were quick enough.

The unnamed man in this verse either had nowhere else to go or he really believed the waters would cure him. He had been trying for some time to get into the pool when the angel stirred the water, but more able-bodied people kept getting there before him, and only one person was allowed in at a time. The frustration level must have been on a par with being seriously ill but not being treated in the emergency room because the doctors were all busy with people complaining of coughs and sniffles.

> *Beautiful Savior, Your ways are not our ways, and they don't need changing or improving. Instead, may we learn to change our ways, our expectations, so they move ever closer to You, no matter how contrary that might seem to common sense. May Your wonderful, unexpected way be the only way, forever and ever. Amen.*

Then Jesus came along and, as always happens when the Lord appears, things changed.

He asked the man if he

would be healed. The man, with his attention still focused on the accepted way of getting better, said he had no one to help him get to the pool in time. Perhaps he envisaged Jesus hanging around until the waters stirred and then carrying him into the water, pushing others aside along the way.

Jesus never even referred to the healing waters. His full attention was on the man before Him. He simply said, "Pick up your bed, and walk." And the man did. Nothing he expected to happen had come to pass, but Jesus had healed him.

The ways of the world can be a trap for the believer as well as the unbeliever. We can both sit around waiting for the expected thing to happen. The believer might think they are doing a good and kind thing helping a troubled soul along the path they are already walking—the equivalent of carrying the man to the pool. It might be kind, but it is also following the ways of the world.

What we need to do above all is somehow introduce Jesus into the equation. Then things will change for the better in ways no one would have expected.

THE STRANGE WOMAN—
The Attire of a Harlot
and a Subtle Heart

And beheld among the simple ones, I discerned among the youths, a young man
void of understanding, passing through the street near her corner; and he went the
way to her house, in the twilight, in the evening, in the black and dark night: and,
behold, there met him a woman with the attire of an harlot, and subtil of heart.

PROVERBS 7:7–10 KJV

The Bible often seems to give women a bad name, painting them as the embodiment of temptation, always leading men astray. Not a very flattering picture of the easily led men either. The man in this proverb is actually described as being "void of understanding."

The woman is left unnamed. She may have been an allegorical figure, but the writer of Proverbs would have met many like her. She was the woman whose restless feet would not allow her to stay at home, the woman who perfumed her bed for another man while her husband was away.

She seems to offer this poor passing fool everything, but the writer compares him to an ox heading to the slaughter. No doubt he will have his moments of pleasure, but the strange woman is described as having destroyed many strong men, and her house described as a way station for hell.

Your adversary is insidious, Lord. Many and complicated are the ways in which he seeks to trap us. We couldn't possibly come up with enough different strategies to escape them all. We are so grateful You provided the Ten Commandments and left us the example of a simple life lived in faith. The devil is in the details, but the life of faith has only two details and there is no space for him in either of them—to love God and love one another.

Leaving aside the sexes—because men can be tempters, too—the issue of temptation is one every Christian faces. It is one of the primary weapons of the enemy. It promises pleasure, which is often enough for the foolish person, but the mature believer knows that a life might be wasted paying for that pleasure. That is the whole point of the affair as far as the devil is concerned; he gambles a few gaudy baubles for the prize of a precious soul.

Financial loan companies these days are often compelled by law to publish their real interest rates. Temptations would not be half as attractive as they currently seem if the devil was compelled to advertise his true rate of return. Unfortunately, he isn't, which is why we all need to walk carefully and choose wisely.

Fortunately, in addition to the woman with the bad name, the Bible also provides some allegorical women with very good names to help with these decisions. Proverbs advises that we "Say unto wisdom, Thou art my sister; and call understanding thy kinswoman" (7:4 KJV).

Now, those are "women" even the most foolish of men would benefit from hanging around with!

THE WOMAN WHO DID
A BEAUTIFUL THING—
Despite the Complaints of Others

While he was in Bethany, reclining at the table in the home of Simon the Leper,
a woman came with an alabaster jar of very expensive perfume, made of
pure nard. She broke the jar and poured the perfume on his head. Some of those
present were saying indignantly to one another, "Why this waste of perfume?
It could have been sold for more than a year's wages and the money
given to the poor." And they rebuked her harshly.

MARK 14:3–5 NIV

The woman who anointed Jesus with nard is both named and unnamed. In the book of John she is identified as Mary, the sister of Lazarus. Matthew and Mark tell similar stories, but they refer to her only as "a woman."

The books of Matthew and Mark were written before John, so this is an interesting anomaly. But we might still learn from the woman's good example, whoever she was.

In honor of a guest whom she loved, who had done wonderful things and who would be leaving them soon, this woman broke open some expensive perfume and rubbed it into Jesus' hair.

> *Lord, may we ever be sources of love and beauty rather than criticism. May we, with Your help, keep our hearts always open to Your possibilities, not ignoring the naysayers but encouraging them to be more trusting, more innocent. May we be creators of beauty in Your beautiful name.*

Perfuming the hair of a guest was a social tradition in those days, but no doubt there were cheaper perfumes available. In her love, this woman gave the best she had. And, of course, "wiser" people complained.

Isn't that always the way? The love that begins

every great work is usually called naive or foolish by the people who "know" it can't be done or think it ought to be done differently.

These changes would never happen if it was left to the critics. It takes a certain amount of innocence and naiveté to have a heart that is open enough to take a chance. Sadly, that open heart often has to quickly grow a thicker skin to protect it from the criticism. Then because it has to protect itself so much the person ends up becoming a critic themselves.

Jesus appreciated this. And He shut the complainers down.

"She has done a beautiful thing to me," He said (verse 6). Beautiful things almost stand alone, exempt by their virtue from the rules that govern lesser acts. He might have added, "And what did you do?" No doubt they would have replied with all the things they might have done with the money the perfume (that they didn't own) could have sold for. But what is any amount of useful things promised compared to one beautiful thing done?

Beauty, if not born of nature, is almost always born of love. And God has a special affinity with love—being its source.

THOSE OF A WILLING HEART—
The Wave Offering for the Tabernacle

Every one that did offer an offering of silver and brass brought the LORD's
offering: and every man, with whom was found shittim wood for any
work of the service, brought it. And all the women that were wise hearted
did spin with their hands, and brought that which they had spun,
both of blue, and of purple, and of scarlet, and of fine linen. And all the
women whose heart stirred them up in wisdom spun goats' hair.
EXODUS 35:24–26 KJV

God had ordered Moses to build Him a house of sorts, a tabernacle in which the Almighty might dwell among and travel with His chosen people.

Well. . .that would have to be one impressive construction job. Moses put the word out that the Lord was coming to stay and the people responded with a "wave offering." In Hebrew tradition, a wave offering is an offering over and above the usual giving, dedicated to a special occasion. But this offering had more in common with a tsunami than a wave. The people gave the best of everything they had, including their time and skills. Eventually they had to be told, "Enough!" They had given more than enough.

Some of the craftsmen, like Bezaleel and Aholiab, are credited for the intricate work they did, but the vast majority of the construction crew—including the women who wove goat hair, spun purple yarn or fine linen, and

> Lord, may we always be willing-hearted and giving when it comes to preparing a place for You in this world—even if the place You want to be is a place we would not willingly choose to go. May we, through our faith and Your provision, make this whole world (or at least our part of it) a suitable tabernacle for the Most High.

dyed the leather—go unnamed. It would hardly have mattered to them. They were preparing for God to come and stay. No amount of personal fame could compete with that.

Moses asked those of a willing heart to give. And everyone did!

The book of Exodus describes the building of the tabernacle at length and in intricate detail. Perhaps uniquely in the accounts of the Bible there is no dissension and nothing went wrong. Everyone played their part willingly and happily. The work of the devil was absent in the building of a house for the Lord. The result—it was a structure that caused Moses to bless the people who had made and decorated it. And the Lord did indeed move in.

If the people "of a willing heart" teach us anything (other than how to build a tabernacle), it is that great and wonderful things can be accomplished when a group of believers get together, putting their own egos and needs aside, to achieve something for God.

Imagine if churches and faith organizations everywhere could follow that example. God might come to stay more often.

THE LEVITE AND
HIS CONCUBINE—
Doing What He Thought Fit

In those days Israel had no king. Now a Levite who lived in a remote area in the hill country of Ephraim took a concubine from Bethlehem in Judah. But she was unfaithful to him. She left him and went back to her parents' home in Bethlehem, Judah. After she had been there four months, her husband went to her to persuade her to return. He had with him his servant and two donkeys. She took him into her parents' home, and when her father saw him, he gladly welcomed him.

JUDGES 19:1–3 NIV

∞∞∞

The story of the anonymous Levite begins with the words, "In those days Israel had no king." It ends with the words, "In those days Israel had no king; everyone did as they saw fit" (Judges 21:25 NIV).

Some might think that a society or a family with no central authority where everyone could do what they wanted would be a good thing. It might be if people were perfect. But they are not.

The Levite, coming from a priestly tradition, should perhaps have tried harder than most to be perfect. But he did not.

For a start, he took a concubine. Throughout the entire sordid tale, there is no mention of his wife. If he had only stayed at home working at being a better husband, the country would have been a safer place.

His concubine ran away from him. Four months later, he pursued her to her father's house. Instead of taking her back immediately (or leaving her there), he stayed for five days getting drunk with her father.

> *Dear Lord, save us from ourselves. We are weak vessels, prone to breaking in different ways, often with disastrous consequences. We need You to hold us together, individually and as a nation. Lord, be our King!*

Traveling on, he refused to spend the night in one city because of tribal loyalties. Instead, he went to another city, Gibeah in Benjamin, where the male inhabitants pounded on the door of the house where he was staying and demanded to have sex with him. It seems his judgment was flawed in more ways than one.

Instead of defying them or leaving, he threw his concubine to them and locked the door. In the morning he woke up and prepared to travel on, without a thought for her. It's only when he opened the door to leave that he found her dead on the doorstep.

Refusing to take any responsibility, in outrage he sent parts of her body to all the tribes of Israel and started a civil war, which all but wiped out the tribe of Benjamin.

The story may have been intended to demonstrate that Israel needed a king, but it also demonstrates how we need a heavenly King in our lives, helping us subdue our troublesome passions and control those selfish attitudes.

Why? Well, because of one man's lust, laziness, indulgence, cowardice, and complete lack of responsibility, thousands died. He would never have considered that his fault, since after all, he was doing what he saw fit. And so was everyone else.

ELISHA'S PARENTS—
A Kiss Then Gone Forever

Elisha then left his oxen and ran after Elijah. "Let me kiss my father and
mother goodbye," he said, "and then I will come with you." "Go back,"
Elijah replied. "What have I done to you?" So Elisha left him and went back.
He took his yoke of oxen and slaughtered them. He burned the plowing
equipment to cook the meat and gave it to the people, and they ate.
Then he set out to follow Elijah and became his servant.

1 KINGS 19:20–21 NIV

Elisha may still be overshadowed somewhat by his predecessor, the prophet Elijah, but he performed twice as many miracles as Elijah did and dedicated his adult life to the service of God. His parents raised a wonderful son, and yet they are hardly credited.

When Elijah appointed him his successor, the young man had only one request—that he be allowed to kiss his parents good-bye. The same scene would be played out centuries later when Jesus apparently rejects a young follower who makes a similar request.

> *Our Father in heaven, children are among the greatest gifts You give to us and one of the greatest responsibilities we will ever know. Give us, please, the patience and the wisdom to raise them in a manner pleasing to their Creator. And, Father God, should You ever ask for them back from us against all worldly expectations, endow us with a joyful heart. May our children be Yours as we are Yours.*

Elijah seems to understand Elisha's sincerity, saying wryly, "What have I done to you?" But it speaks volumes about their relationship that he made the request in the midst of his excitement.

Elisha kissed his parents, then said a farewell that left no possibility of a return to his old life. We never hear of his parents again. They obviously didn't object or follow after him weeping and wailing. It seems that this was the role they raised him for—and he loved them for it.

They may have seen him about his work from time to time, but from that point on he was God's man.

We read on occasion in the Bible of children being dedicated to God from birth. It's a less fashionable option these days, and deciding what kind of an adult a child will become is often a gamble. But that doesn't mean we should let our children grow up like weeds.

Some discipline and direction are always useful, and it is up to us to provide it if we raise them in a godly household. But we must be prepared, as Elisha's parents seem to have been, to lose them temporarily to the God who gave them to us in the first place. When they want to go out and make a difference for good in the world, kiss them and let them go. The world may not ever know your name, but you will know you made the most of the gift you were given.

THE SHUNAMMITE WOMAN—
It's Not About Her Son

One day Elisha went to Shunem. And a well-to-do woman was there, who urged
him to stay for a meal. So whenever he came by, he stopped there to eat.
She said to her husband, "I know that this man who often comes our way is a holy
man of God. Let's make a small room on the roof and put in it a bed and a table,
a chair and a lamp for him. Then he can stay there whenever he comes to us."

2 KINGS 4:8–10 NIV

The story of the unnamed Shunammite woman usually focuses on
how God (through Elisha) granted her a son when she had none.
Then, the unnamed son seems to die and Elisha rushed to restore him
to life. Understandably, the birth, death, and resurrection would seem
to be the whole point of the story.

But there is another less dramatic lesson to be drawn from the
tale, one we can all relate to.

Elisha was a doughty man of God, and as such, he knew more
than his fair share of troubled times. But, there was one place in
Shunem where he was usually guaranteed a friendly welcome, some
rest and some refreshment.

> We pray, "Thy will be done, in
> heaven as on earth," so we should
> be willing to see it done on earth.
> More than that, Lord, we should
> be prepared to make sure it gets
> done. After all, what are our
> resources but gifts from You? May
> we have the heart to give at least
> some of them back to Your service.

The Shunammite was
a wealthy woman who had
taken to feeding Elisha
whenever he was in town.
Then she went further.
Recognizing that Elisha
was a man constantly about
God's business—and often
too busy to worry about
domestic arrangements—
with the agreement of her

husband, she had a new room built on the roof of their house and had it dressed with comfortable furniture. This was to be Elisha's home away from home when he was in Shunem.

The gifts and kindness such as she showed Elisha would have been rare and beautiful occurrences in an otherwise austere life.

Not everyone can build an extension to their house for a visiting pastor, but we can each follow the Shunammite woman's example in our own way, according to our own abilities. The question we need to ask is this: Is there any part of our home, income, or life that we can dedicate to God in a practical way? What we lack in resources we might make up for in initiative.

Whatever it turns out to be will depend on you, but, like the Shunammite woman, you should make it a permanent and public fixture in your life. Do that in a spirit of service and devotion and, to paraphrase the movie *Field of Dreams*, you will find that "If you build it. . .God will come."

PETER'S MOTHER-IN-LAW—
What She Did Differently

And when Jesus was come into Peter's house, he saw his wife's mother laid,
and sick of a fever. And he touched her hand, and the fever left her:
and she arose, and ministered unto them.
MATTHEW 8:14–15 KJV

To say Jesus was busy at this time would be an understatement.

He had just preached what came to be known as the Sermon on the Mount. Coming off the crowded hillside He healed a man of leprosy, then He saved the centurion's servant, then He made Peter's mother-in-law well, and later that day, He drove out several demons. Not a bad day's work.

And what did He get out of it all, apart from the satisfaction of doing His Father's will?

He got a few thank-yous. But only one person did anything for Him in return.

When He arrived at His disciple Peter's house, they found his mother-in-law in bed, sick. Jesus reached out, touched her, and she was healed! She must have heard of Jesus' miracles, but it would still have been a shock to be on the receiving end of one.

She didn't simply thank the Lord. She didn't rush off to tell everyone about the encounter. She immediately began waiting on her guest. No doubt she washed His

> *Dear Lord, all too often we let the fact that we can't do much stop us from doing anything. But just as simple souls with simple faith were Your priority, so we might make simple service ours. We never know when what we have to offer might mean the world to the recipient. It isn't required of us that we know. It is simply our part to do what we can in a spirit of love—and leave the rest to You.*

feet, brought Him food, and did whatever else she could.

Admittedly, this was normal hospitality. But she, as the elder woman of the house, would have been able to delegate those duties to her daughter, especially as she had so recently been ill. But she didn't. It was nothing more than Jesus might have expected as a guest to the house, but that doesn't mean her simple services weren't a blessing to the Lord on an otherwise hectic day.

Peter's mother-in-law did that very rare—and now impossible—thing. She gave something back to Jesus!

When we compare the number of people Jesus helped in His earthly ministry with the times we know about when people helped Him, this woman's hospitality stands out.

Sadly, we will never be given that opportunity (in this life at least), but we can do the next best thing. If we are at all aware of the miracles Jesus has done for us and the blessings the Lord has scattered over our lives, then we might want to give something back, as well. While we can't serve Jesus directly, we can show kindness and hospitality to the ones He loves.

What's the best way to do that? Just as Peter's mother-in-law did—through simple service.

PHARAOH'S DAUGHTER—
A Pagan Princess "Mothers" the Hebrew Nation

And the daughter of Pharaoh came down to wash herself at the river;
and her maidens walked along by the river's side; and when she saw
the ark among the flags, she sent her maid to fetch it. And when she
had opened it, she saw the child: and, behold, the babe wept. And she
had compassion on him, and said, This is one of the Hebrews' children.

EXODUS 2:5–6 KJV

God once used the king of the pagan Assyrians as a tool to scourge an unfaithful nation. Why could He not then use a pagan princess to help renew it?

The pharaoh ruling in Egypt at the time was not a friend to the Hebrew population living in his country. He, or his advisers, feared they were becoming too numerous and might outnumber the Egyptians if war broke out, so he decreed that newborn Hebrew boys be killed. Despite the best efforts of the Hebrew mothers and their midwives, many children died as result of this decree.

That alone tells us all we need to know about this pharaoh. His daughter, however, seemed to have been an altogether finer specimen of a person. She must have known about the decree and she obviously knew that the baby in the basket floating in the Nile was a Hebrew, but she defied her father's wishes

> *Heavenly Father, laws will come and go, and we strive much to obey the law of the land. But some laws are eternal, and we owe our first allegiance to them. May we always follow Your laws, those written in the Ten Commandments, those taught to us by Your Son, Jesus Christ, and those You have written in our hearts. Amen.*

to let baby Moses live. To do otherwise would probably have broken this young woman's heart (as hearts must have been breaking among the Hebrews).

Perhaps she used the time she left the baby with his natural mother to work on softening her father's heart—because, sometime afterward, she was able to adopt Moses into the Egyptian royal family.

Moses grew to manhood as a prince of Egypt thanks to the kindness of his adoptive mother. There he grew strong and was well educated. Who knows what he might have become if pity for his own people hadn't caused him to lead them out of Egypt?

But his fate was set. He would be a father of a nation, leading God's people to their new home. So, Israel has a lot to thank this pagan princess for. Without her, there would have been no Moses to lead the Exodus. Doubtless God would have raised someone else up, but her kind heart meant He didn't have to.

So, what can we who aren't royalty learn from this noble lady? Perhaps that nobility doesn't lie in an accident of birth—it lies in how you treat other people. Or, perhaps that love should be the ruling factor in our lives, even when great powers are arrayed against it. Because there is no greater power than love.

THE DAUGHTERS OF PRIESTS—
Of Whom More Was Expected

" 'They must not marry women defiled by prostitution or divorced from
their husbands, because priests are holy to their God. Regard them as holy,
because they offer up the food of your God. Consider them holy, because I the
LORD am holy—I who make you holy. If a priest's daughter defiles herself by
becoming a prostitute, she disgraces her father; she must be burned in the fire.' "
LEVITICUS 21:7–9 NIV

Some verses of the Bible, especially in the harsher times of the Old Testament, can make unpleasant reading for a modern audience, but we must strive to learn from them all the same.

Much was given to the priests of the Hebrew nation—but much was asked of them. As God's representatives on earth, only the highest of standards were expected from them. These standards were also expected of the priest's family, whether they agreed or not. In those days, a man's children and wife were not greatly differentiated from his possessions. What he said or did set the rule for the whole family.

Many a modern minister's son or daughter has rebelled against the religious life and brought shame and hurt to the family. But they would not expect to be executed for it!

Becoming a prostitute in this instance didn't actually mean setting yourself up as a "working girl." It just meant ignoring the sexual and social expectations of the time. The daughter of an ordinary family could be strangled for adultery. The daughter of a priest would be made to suffer more—she would be burned.

> *Dear God, we do our best for You and our brothers and sisters, but we can never hope to attain Your standards. But it is the trying that brings us ever closer to You.*

If we can draw no lessons from the horrific

punishments, we might still learn a little from the expectations. The family was associated with the priest. The priest was associated with God. If God is holy, then it might not be unnatural to expect those closest to Him to be holier than those who lived one step removed.

These days, however, thanks to the intervention of Jesus Christ our Lord, we have a direct relationship with God. He isn't going to execute us if we don't live up to His standards. If we repent of our sin, He will forgive us, and despite anything we do, He will keep on loving us.

So, the least we can do in return is voluntarily raise our standards and live in such a way that He will be pleased.

And one other thing: we ought to remember there are many out there who don't know about God. We can help them best by standing out from the crowd. If we are people of God, then people searching for Him ought to be able to look around and see Him in us, to see how we are directly associated with a wonderful God and how His love encourages us to live up to a wonderful standard.

THE TABERNACLE WOMEN—
Defenseless but Not
without a Champion

*So he said to them, "Why do you do such things? I hear from all the people
about these wicked deeds of yours. No, my sons; the report I hear spreading
among the LORD's people is not good. If one person sins against another,
God may mediate for the offender; but if anyone sins against the LORD,
who will intercede for them?" His sons, however, did not listen to their
father's rebuke, for it was the LORD's will to put them to death.*

1 SAMUEL 2:23–25 NIV

⸺⸺

Eli was a good and faithful high priest, but he was a poor and ineffectual father. It would be the undoing of his family as well as the promise God made that Eli's descendants would be priests forever. Fortunately, he was a better adoptive father to his successor Samuel than he was to his natural sons.

Hophni and Phinehas had been born and raised in a life of privilege. As the sons of the high priest they automatically became priests themselves, no matter what their personal qualities. That meant they had free access to all the offerings made to God by the people and authority over everyone else who served in the tabernacle.

Hophni and Phinehas took full advantage of their position. Their families grew fat from the food that should have become burnt offerings. And, despite being married men, they also took advantage

> *Father God, help us to follow the
> example of the good tabernacle
> servants and live lives of purity.
> Teach us to value it in all its
> forms because it affords us a
> glimpse of You and Your plan for
> us. One day we will be purified.
> Until then, may we always be
> supporters and defenders of
> purity—never its defilers.*

of the women who served in the sanctuary.

Their actions would, no doubt, have constituted repeated rape. Usually the people who served in the tabernacle or the temple were consecrated to God by their families when they were children. Their families would then have little or no contact with them for the rest of their lives. Tabernacle workers could also be foundlings living off God's charity. These women most likely had no one to defend them. And in a country ruled by priests, Phinehas and Hophni had all the power. There was no one but Eli to hold them to account, and he got there too late.

The women may not have had a protector at the time, but they did have someone willing to avenge them. God revoked the right of the family of Eli to serve Him as priest and saw to it that the two main offenders were killed in battle. Upon hearing the news, Eli, who certainly bore some of the responsibility, fell off his chair and died.

Perhaps God was avenging the desecration of His tabernacle, but He also was avenging the women who had been taken advantage of in the midst of their holy service to Him; as part of the tabernacle's life, their purity was seen as holy.

God values purity. He does not value those who desecrate it.

ABIGAIL'S SERVING WOMEN—
Where She Went, They Went

His servants went to Carmel and said to Abigail, "David has sent us to you to take you to become his wife." She bowed down with her face to the ground and said, "I am your servant and am ready to serve you and wash the feet of my lord's servants." Abigail quickly got on a donkey and, attended by her five female servants, went with David's messengers and became his wife.

1 SAMUEL 25:40–42 NIV

We know nothing about Abigail's female servants other than she took them with her when she went to marry King David. They had served the family under her previous husband, Nabal (whom she didn't always get on with), and King David would have been willing to supply her with plenty of servants, perhaps ones better trained for royal life.

It was the ideal chance to leave her old life behind her—but she took them with her. We can only assume they were good servants and she valued them. Perhaps she thought of them as family. But she was the one who had control over their futures. Wherever she decreed, they would go.

Time and again through the Bible, we hear of servants living their lives where and how their masters and mistresses commanded. Slavery was legal at the time, and there were laws in place to give some protection. But many people, both then and now, lived lives where they had no control over what the world might call the

> Our hearts, Lord, are where we feel You dwell and where we feel the absence most when You seem distant from us. May they be our greatest gift to You, a place for You to rest, the place where You might comfort us when all the world seems against us. May those hearts always be free in Your love, even supposing our bodies are in captivity. Amen.

most important aspects of their lives.

What are we to learn from them? How should we behave if we are one of them?

Some—like the servant of Naaman's wife, who was a spoil of war—performed service for God. Joseph, who was sold as a slave, rose to great power. But most simply did the best they could wherever they happened to be. If there was peace and contentment in their lives, it had to come from some source other than personal control. You might say it had to be found in surrender.

The little things of life done in prayer and devotion can be as much a service to God as the bigger things. The seventeenth-century Carmelite monk Brother Lawrence used to mend sandals and wash dishes to the best of his abilities, giving even those menial tasks as offerings to God.

What Abigail's servants and many others teach us is that the world might control our lives but only we control our hearts, and if we choose, even in captivity, to turn them toward the Lord, He will receive them as a precious offering.

JONATHAN'S ARMOR-BEARER—
A Trainee Man of God

Jonathan said to his young armor-bearer, "Come, let's go over to the outpost of those uncircumcised men. Perhaps the LORD will act in our behalf. Nothing can hinder the LORD from saving, whether by many or by few." "Do all that you have in mind," his armor-bearer said. "Go ahead; I am with you heart and soul."

1 SAMUEL 14:6–7 NIV

⸺⸙⸺

Jonathan, son of Saul, was one of the noblest men in the Bible. He loved the Lord and was true to his friends; he was a servant of his king and a brave man in war. He would die in battle beside a father who did not deserve his loyalty.

One of his most notable exploits also involved a young armor-bearer. Jonathan decided to climb a cliff to see if there were Philistines at the top. He had no way of knowing how many there might be, but he was sure that he and his armor-bearer would stand or fall on God's will no matter how outnumbered they were. The young armor-bearer had known Jonathan long enough to place complete trust in him.

There were twenty men at the top of that cliff and they knew Jonathan was coming, but he and his armor-bearer killed all of them.

> *Lord, we thank You for allowing each and every one of us to carry and wear the armor of God in our times of need. You are the Master of masters, but we will always be prepared to learn from those You place before us. Then may we have the pleasure of passing Your protection on to some younger "soldier" of the Lord.*

An armor-bearer was almost like an apprentice soldier. He would go into battle behind his master carrying the array of weapons that might be needed and was prepared to supply them the second they were required. This way, the master was more agile and more able to concentrate on tactical fighting. Despite being loaded with weaponry, they were usually solely dependent on their master for protection. They often went on to make excellent soldiers, having studied the art of war so often from such close quarters.

We should pray that fewer young men and women find themselves fighting wars these days. But even in peacetime, it helps to follow someone like Jonathan—an older man or woman more advanced in the faith—so we might learn from them. And if we can lighten their load, whether it be by stacking seats after a meeting or doing necessary research, then we might leave them free to do more of God's work—which has to be a victory. Then, by learning the "art of faith" at close quarters, we might someday be able to teach others.

The skills of the armor-bearer have not disappeared from the world. It's just that these days they involve more digital presentations and long drives to seminars than knowing how to handle an ax safely or carry a spear on the run without tripping over it.

THE MOTHER OF
JAMES AND JOHN—
Humble for Greatness

*Then the mother of Zebedee's sons came to Jesus with her sons and, kneeling
down, asked a favor of him. "What is it you want?" he asked. She said,
"Grant that one of these two sons of mine may sit at your right and the other at
your left in your kingdom." "You don't know what you are asking," Jesus said to
them. "Can you drink the cup I am going to drink?" "We can," they answered.*
MATTHEW 20:20–22 NIV

———◆———

The wife of Zebedee unconsciously took one of Jesus' teachings and
made a mockery of it. She approached Jesus and knelt before Him,
begging a favor. The favor wasn't for herself. She would just really
appreciate it if Jesus would raise one of her boys, either James or
John—she didn't mind which—to sit at the right hand of the Lord
in heaven.

Presumptuous? Yes. And possibly very dangerous considering
what Jesus would have to go
through before He would sit on
His heavenly throne again.

She wasn't asking for herself
. . .but as a mother, would she
not have enjoyed basking in such
familial glory? The achievement
would have been hers, no matter
which son was chosen. No matter how humble she appeared on
her knees, she was aiming for old-
fashioned greatness, a heavenly
dynasty perhaps.

What Jesus was busy teaching

> *Lord, we act and speak
> foolishly at times. All too
> often we know not what we
> do. Forgive us our pointless
> desire and meaningless
> ambitions. May our prayers to
> You be conversation of either
> real need or enthusiastic
> appreciation, trusting that
> You have everything else in
> hand. May we, in our hearts,
> be Yours to place where You
> need us when You need us.*

was that the glory inherent in humility was its own reward, and those who were considered greatest in heaven would be those who gave with no thought of receiving.

Zebedee's wife might have claimed there was nothing in it for her—but she was still driven by parental ambition. She didn't mind if the other disciples heard about her request, and they weren't happy when they did. Ambition so often breeds division.

Scholars speculate that this unnamed woman was actually Salome, one of the women at the foot of the cross. If so, we can only suppose she learned true humility along the way and that Jesus became dearer to her than any ambition.

Perhaps at that terrible time, she remembered the favor she asked and was relieved that neither of her sons were at His right or left hand.

As for the rest of us, we can paraphrase the instructions the Lord used to calm the quarrelsome disciples after the woman's request. It is the people without faith who lord their position over others. God's people will be there at the foot of the cross or at the feet of the needy, serving others for the glory of God rather than their own fame.

THE GUARDS AT THE TOMB—
Like Dead Men

"Sir," they said, "we remember that while he was still alive that deceiver said, 'After three days I will rise again.' So give the order for the tomb to be made secure until the third day. Otherwise, his disciples may come and steal the body and tell the people that he has been raised from the dead. This last deception will be worse than the first." "Take a guard," Pilate answered. "Go, make the tomb as secure as you know how."
MATTHEW 27:63–65 NIV

———

After the crucifixion, the chief priests were afraid the disciples would make it seem as if Jesus had risen by stealing away His body, so they requested guards be placed at the tomb. Despite His many miracles, they don't seem to have considered the possibility that He might actually rise.

But what kind of men were these guards?

Because they were dispatched by Pilate, we can be sure they were Roman soldiers. Because Palestine during the Roman occupation was a volatile place, we can assume they were battle hardened. Whether they were prepared to stand watch at a dead man's tomb all night, we can only wonder. It would be no surprise if they fell asleep either through heavenly intervention or through sheer boredom.

If it was the latter, it wasn't to last. The earthquake probably started them shaking from fear, and a visit from a glowing angel probably shook them into unconsciousness.

> *Lord, in You there is only life, and that is a gift we have only begun to explore. Preserve us from self-delusion that we may see, our eyes widening in amazement, all You have done for us and all You have planned for us. May we be alive in You—and abundantly so!*

Whatever caused it, they "became like dead men" (Matthew 28:4 NIV).

While these warriors lay on the ground, the tomb was emptied.

The Bible says they reported everything that happened to the priests, who then bribed them to tell another story. You have to wonder at the length to which some people will go to remain unbelievers. The priests must have believed the soldiers—who must have been embarrassed to recount such a tale—but despite the fact that the powers of heaven were obviously working against them, they all agreed to carry on as if nothing had changed.

The soldiers were paid a large sum of money for their cooperation, perhaps even enough to buy themselves out of the army. But we wonder what effect the encounter had on them in later years. Did they find themselves drawn to the church in Rome seeking an explanation? Or did they keep on ignoring heaven and everything associated with it? What a desolate life that would be.

In ignoring the obvious power of the Almighty and every good thing associated with it, those Roman soldiers must have spent the rest of their lives almost like the time they spent on the ground before the empty tomb—like dead men.

THE DEMON IN
THE SYNAGOGUE—
"I Know Who You Are!"

Just then a man in their synagogue who was possessed by an impure
spirit cried out, "What do you want with us, Jesus of Nazareth?
Have you come to destroy us? I know who you are—the Holy One of God!"
"Be quiet!" said Jesus sternly. "Come out of him!" The impure spirit
shook the man violently and came out of him with a shriek.

MARK 1:23–26 NIV

⸻⸻

Soon after His baptism Jesus was teaching in Capernaum when a
demon-possessed man called Him out as the Holy One of God.
Given that it was early in His ministry, it is perhaps odd that the
forces of evil would identify Him publicly while He insisted on
keeping it quiet.

You would have to wonder why anyone doubted His identity
afterward.

Because the man was in the synagogue and synagogues tend to
be community places where everyone knows each other, the demon
had either lain quiet in this man for a while or suddenly come upon
him. We have no way of knowing which. But the questions it asked
were appropriate to both the demon and the man: What do you want
with us? Have you come here to destroy us?

Jesus hadn't come to destroy demons even though He cast
many out of their human hosts. If God had wished them destroyed,
He could have done so without

> *Wonderful Savior, You meet*
> *us where we are, in whatever*
> *condition we may be. You ask*
> *the best of us and the worst of*
> *us to follow You. May we always*
> *say yes and may we be delighted*
> *rather than surprised by the*
> *company we find ourselves in.*

sending His Son. Jesus had come to save humanity.

He hadn't come to destroy the man either, but for many of the Jews it would seem like He was at least trying to destroy their way of life.

Jesus was always a man of contradictions. He can be a gift or a challenge depending on your attitude and whether you are prepared to accept Him or not. The man in the synagogue might have been grateful to have a demon cast out of him—or he might have been embarrassed. He may have become a follower—or he may have played a part in an established order that resisted even the evidence of their own experience in order to discredit a man they feared.

We have to wonder what he told his wife that night when she asked how his day had been.

The questions the man in the synagogue asked are still valid today. The answer will depend on where we stand with God, on whether we are willing to accept His gift of eternity or remain willing prisoners of this transient world who want nothing to do with Him.

What do You want from us? Are You here to destroy us?

To those of us willing to meet Him in love, the answers are, "All of you," and, "No, I am here to restore you."

THE MEN OF LYSTRA—
Doing a New Thing the Old Way

In Lystra there sat a man who was lame. He had been that way from birth
and had never walked. He listened to Paul as he was speaking. Paul looked
directly at him, saw that he had faith to be healed and called out, "Stand up on
your feet!" At that, the man jumped up and began to walk.

ACTS 14:8–10 NIV

Paul and Barnabas had been having a tough time on their mission
tour. They had fled Iconium for their own safety, but things seemed to
improve when they arrived in Lystra.

A "simple" miracle—the healing of a lame man—had greatly
impressed the populace of the city. People who had never heard
such preaching before suddenly began enthusing over the Gospel.
But then things started to go too far. These new "converts" insisted
Paul and Barnabas were not merely representatives of God but were
actually gods themselves. And not just any old gods, but Hermes and
Zeus. A priest of Zeus even brought livestock to sacrifice to them.

Paul managed to convince the men of Lystra that he and Barnabas
were normal human beings. He tried again to tell them about Jesus,
but by this point some of the people who had turned against the
apostles in Iconium had appeared. The confused men of Lystra went
from hero-worship to serious assault in no time. They stoned Paul
and dumped him outside the city walls.

People often like to think they are open-minded. They will assure you they are prepared to accept new ideas. But when the time comes, they prefer to

Lord, my life before You was so
wrong in so many ways. May I
forget it like You forget my forgiven
sins. Take this new me and make
me what You will. In You and
Your ways will I trust.

package them in old, familiar ways so they can say they have changed without actually doing anything different.

The easily swayed men of Lystra were like that. They loved the message and the miracles Paul and Barnabas brought but preferred to wrap them up in old, familiar traditions. When the apostles would not let them do that and they were faced with having to accept a message that was radically different, well. . . That's when things got ugly.

It's not a trait peculiar to those long-gone men of Lystra. Even today people come to faith and the outside observer would be unable to tell that it made any difference in their lives. The habits of old are difficult to break, but while we cling to them we allow no room for Jesus in our hearts. If Jesus is not in our hearts, then no one will know whether we are in faith or not by looking at our lives.

The message of the Gospel is one of change and freedom from the old way. If you don't like it, don't stone the messenger! But if you do, accept it will change you for the better—and change you forever!

THE TAX COLLECTORS
AND SINNERS—
The Doctor Calls

When the teachers of the law who were Pharisees saw him eating with the sinners and tax collectors, they asked his disciples: "Why does he eat with tax collectors and sinners?" On hearing this, Jesus said to them, "It is not the healthy who need a doctor, but the sick. I have not come to call the righteous, but sinners."
MARK 2:16–17 NIV

Levi had been quietly collecting his taxes when Jesus wandered by and invited Himself and a whole lot of friends to dinner. It's a good thing Levi had been taking more than his wages from the taxes he collected. That would have been one expensive meal! To his credit, he never seemed to have hesitated.

Pretty soon the Pharisees came wandering by. Jesus must have thought those guys followed Him everywhere (because they probably did). Their facial expressions would have spoken volumes when they saw this man who claimed to be a spiritual teacher dining with sinners and tax collectors.

This was business as usual as far as those sinners were concerned. That kind of derision was what they were used to. They experienced it from people like the Pharisees on a daily basis. The unusual thing for them would have been sitting down to eat with a man who wasn't one of them and still didn't judge them.

They must have been judged and found wanting every day of their lives. Is it any wonder they never considered another way of life? The condemnation of

> *Lord, not judging is difficult. Remind us when we are tempted to judge others that we may be closing the door in their minds that leads to You. May we always be the open door that allows others through to You.*

"righteous" men would never have allowed it.

In Jesus' company, a new life was not only possible; it was actually what He was all about. Imagine how refreshing that felt to their world-weary souls.

The reason Jesus commanded us not to judge may well have been because doing so shuts so many doors, closes down so many possibilities. Sinners have already closed a lot of doors in their own lives by their actions, and society closes many more in its disapproval. To sit and talk with someone who brought out the best in them, who treated them as children of God, must have been powerful medicine to these "sick" souls.

Of course, the sinners and tax collectors might have comforted themselves with one thought. Jesus described Himself as a doctor who had come to heal the sick. He was sitting with them—which suggested they might have been His intended patients—but He seemed to think the oh-so-superior Pharisees were already hopeless cases.

Those of us alive today might read the story of Jesus eating with the sinners and tax collectors and wish we could dine in such wonderful company. Well, we can. Invite a few of society's various outcasts to dinner—and Jesus will surely come along, too.

THE MAN WITH THE
WITHERED HAND—
Between Good and Evil

Another time Jesus went into the synagogue, and a man with a shriveled
hand was there. Some of them were looking for a reason to accuse Jesus,
so they watched him closely to see if he would heal him on the Sabbath.
Jesus said to the man with the shriveled hand, "Stand up in front of everyone."
Then Jesus asked them, "Which is lawful on the Sabbath: to do good or to do evil,
to save life or to kill?" But they remained silent.
MARK 3:1–4 NIV

Jesus, knowing how the Pharisees operated, decided to turn the tables on them. They had presented Him with a sinner (the woman caught in adultery) to see if He would condemn her according to the law. Now He presented them with a man with a withered hand and asked whether it was lawful to heal him on the Sabbath.

They, of course, had their own ideas—fixed for centuries—of what was and was not allowed on the Sabbath, but to say He could not heal this man would paint them as the heartless hypocrites they mostly were. They enforced laws given for the "good" of the people at the expense of those same people, enhancing their own authority in the process. Jesus prioritized the people at the expense of the stricter interpretations of the laws.

In this instance, Jesus actually presented it as a battle between good and evil.

Epic philosophical battles like that are important, of course, but

> Lord, we are commanded to obey the laws of the land, but sometimes flawed laws are written for wrong reasons. How are we to know which we should obey? In times of doubt, may we decide according to the amount of good they do our fellow man in his time of need.

nowhere near as important as the poor man caught in the middle. The man probably wasn't all that bothered by which day of the week he was healed on. His withered hand probably meant he couldn't work. If he couldn't work, his family would go hungry. He may have been reduced to begging on the streets because of his disability.

Healing was probably a much bigger deal to him than either side winning this argument.

Of course, Jesus heals him and called the Pharisees' bluff. Thoroughly humiliated, they leave and then these supposedly righteous men start planning how they will kill Jesus.

But this, too, is part of God's plan.

While all these grand designs were being played out, the man with the withered hand—which was now perfectly healthy—probably celebrated. He may have caressed his wife's hair with the once-useless hand or stroked a child's face. Hopefully, he gave thanks to Jesus.

The people in these stories are what it is all about. The Bible can seem like the unveiling of God's great plan, but God's great plan is to love and save the human race, maybe even one at a time.

THE ROOF DIGGERS—
Any Way to Jesus

Some men came, bringing to him a paralyzed man, carried by four of them.
Since they could not get him to Jesus because of the crowd, they made
an opening in the roof above Jesus by digging through it and then
lowered the mat the man was lying on. When Jesus saw their faith,
he said to the paralyzed man, "Son, your sins are forgiven."
MARK 2:3–5 NIV

The paralyzed man was twice saved. He was redeemed of his sins, and he was sent home walking. But what of the four men who brought him to the Savior? How strong must their faith have been?

We don't know how far they carried him, but people traveled long distances to see Jesus in those days.

We know they could work as a team, so it's a reasonable guess that the paralyzed man was once part of their team—a part they wouldn't leave behind.

They didn't let the crowd that had gathered to see the Lord stop them. When they couldn't get in by the door, they hoisted their friend up onto the roof. How difficult must it have been to get a paralyzed man and his stretcher onto a roof? Presumably they found no ready-made access on the roof, so they started digging. Any roof strong enough to take the weight of four men would be a solid one, probably made of dried mud or clay.

Lord, we have faith, but we are also prone to doubts, and sometimes those doubts can be overwhelming. We know who plants those doubts in our minds, but we can't help being affected by them. Do some digging in our hearts, Lord, and pull out the weeds of doubt so we may come closer to You in faith—by whatever means possible.

Imagine the scene from the crowded room below when the paralyzed man was lowered down! He suddenly became the focus of all the attention, but he would never have gotten there if it hadn't been for the four friends still up on the roof (presumably hoping it would still support them after all their digging!).

If they hadn't been so determined, they might have worried about taking a paralyzed man into such a crowd; they might have worried about the reaction of the homeowner to their "vandalism"; they might have thought Jesus would think them foolish or irreverent.

All the worries that stop us from bringing people to Christ even now.

But they weren't concerned about how they looked or whether they would get into trouble or not. They were concerned only about their friend and getting him to the Man they knew without a doubt could heal him. If they had harbored any doubts, they would never have gotten as far as they did.

The roof diggers present a constant challenge to the rest of us. Across the centuries they ask the question—how far would you go to bring someone to Christ?

THE COUPLE AT CANA—
The Best Possible Start

On the third day a wedding took place at Cana in Galilee. Jesus' mother
was there, and Jesus and his disciples had also been invited to the wedding.
When the wine was gone, Jesus' mother said to him, "They have no more wine."
"Woman, why do you involve me?" Jesus replied. "My hour has not yet come."
His mother said to the servants, "Do whatever he tells you."
JOHN 2:1–5 NIV

⸻

Jesus' baptism by John signaled the beginning of His earthly mission, so you would imagine there was a lot of important stuff to do. According to the book of John, Jesus spent the next day gathering many of His disciples around Him, and on the day after that. . . They took time off to go to a wedding!

We don't know who the happy couple was, but they seem to have been favorites of Mary, the mother of Jesus. Mary seems to have been the important invitee, while Jesus and His disciples (men He had only met the day before) were "also invited." Perhaps they didn't actually know the couple and it was Mary who invited them along.

Why would she do such a thing? Perhaps because this young couple starting out in matrimony was dear to her. Perhaps she knew their families were struggling to afford a proper wedding feast. Perhaps she wanted to give them every chance at success and invited along the most supportive people she knew.

That's a lot of supposition. But the fact is the wedding party did run out of wine. It would have been a disgrace if the lack were discovered. And

> *Dear Lord, as much as I value having You in my life, I deeply desire to share You with others. Answer my prayers, if You will, on behalf of those I love, those who hate me, and those I wish would come to know You for themselves. Amen.*

the man who could fix that for them just happened to be there, even if He was a little reluctant to get involved.

His mother gently ignored His protestations that He wasn't ready and told the servants to do as He instructed. If the quality of the wine He produced from jugs of plain water was anything to go by, the rest of the wedding feast would have been a great success.

We don't know any more about the young newlyweds (although we can assume Mary kept an eye on them). We could hope they were entirely oblivious to the whole wine debacle, having eyes only for each other. But we do know they had a friend who was prepared to intercede with Jesus for their sake, so we might safely assume that many other prayers on their behalf were answered.

What better gift could anyone bring along to a wedding—or a baptism, or an illness, or a house of grief, or a birthday celebration, or a visit to a friend, or a meeting with an enemy—than Jesus Christ our Savior?

SCRIPTURE INDEX

New Testament

ABOUT THE AUTHOR

David McLaughlan stood at the ocean's edge hoping the storm would blow his soul clean again. His work had taken him to some pretty dark places. So, he asked God for help.

From that point on, he decided, his life and work should revolve around the three things that mattered most to him—faith, family, and friendship. Almost immediately God opened a door for him with Barbour Publishing and since then he has written, or contributed to, more books and devotionals than he can remember.

Writing about the "three fs" will never make him rich—but it does make his heart sing! He describes himself as "blessed beyond all reasonable expectation."

He lives in bonnie Scotland with Julie (who first encouraged him to pursue the dream of being a writer) and a whole "clan" of children. Although, as the American branch of the family keeps producing beautiful grandchildren, they find themselves more and more often in the States.

He writes a Sunday newspaper column in the UK encouraging people to find the extra in the ordinary. That "extra" is, of course, always God.